PALACES
OF THE PEOPLE

A SOCIAL HISTORY OF COMMERCIAL HOSPITALITY

ARTHUR WHITE

D0524155

Rapp & Whiting London

With affectionate regards
to Chris and Peter,
in whose lovely home
this book was started.

© ARTHUR WHITE 1968
FIRST PUBLISHED 1968 BY
RAPP AND WHITING LIMITED
76 NEW OXFORD STREET LONDON WCI
PRINTED IN GREAT BRITAIN BY
THE GARDEN CITY PRESS LIMITED
AT LETCHWORTH HERTFORDSHIRE

CONTENTS

ACKNOWLEDGEMENTS

The extract from *Two Middle Aged Ladies in Andalucia* by Penelope Chetwode on pages 25 and 26 is quoted by kind permission of John Murray (Publishers) Limited. The photographs are acknowledged as follows:

Paul Popper Ltd: facing pages 20, 21, 52 (top), 53, 85 (top) 117 (bottom).

Tourist Photo Library Ltd: facing pages 84, 85 (bottom), 116 (bottom), 117 (top).

Shepherd's Hotel: facing page 52 (bottom).

PLATES

1766 — U.S.A.

"A weary and hungry traveller on a jaded horse rode up to the door of a tavern and asked to stay the night. The landlady having assented, the following ensued:

Traveller: Have you provender for my horse?

Landlady: No, we have none.

Traveller: Can you furnish me with supper?

Landlady: We have no bread. My husband started for the mill this morning and will return tomorrow.

Traveller: Can you furnish me with a glass of whisky?

Landlady: We have none. My husband took his gallon bottle and will bring some when he returns.

Traveller: Madam, can you tell me what you do for the entertainment of travellers?

Landlady: We keep a tavern, sir."

"Old Times" Le Roy Journal.

1966 — GREAT BRITAIN

"True dialogue from Blackpool" (Conservative Party Conference).

Tory Central Office Person to Hotel Receptionist: I'd like some sandwiches to take up to my room.

Receptionist: Sorry, we haven't got any sandwiches.

T.C.O.P.: Well, let me have some bread then.

Receptionist: Sorry, we haven't got any bread either.

T.C.O.P.: I think I'd better have a word with the manager.

Receptionist: Sorry, the manager doesn't speak to guests.

Nigel Lawson, "Notebook" *Spectator* 21.10.66.

AUTHOR'S NOTE

SINCE Chaucer wrote up *The Tabard* there has always been a great affinity between the writer and the hostelry.

> There is no private house in which people can enjoy themselves so well as at a capital tavern. Let there be ever so great plenty of good things, ever so much elegance, ever so much desire that everybody should be easy, in the nature of things it cannot be, there must always be some degree of care and anxiety . . . there is nothing which has yet been contrived by man by which so much happiness is produced as by a good tavern or inn.

It was a sweeping statement of Johnson's but in the two centuries since he made it has anything better been contrived? Generally speaking the literary world appears to think not. Hilaire Belloc stated flatly, "When you have lost your inns drown your empty selves, for you will have lost the last of England." On a more expensive level Arnold Bennett had a love affair with the Savoy in exactly the same way as Marcel Proust had with the Ritz in Paris.

Romanticised by Dickens, glamorised by Bennett, eulogised by Chesterton, and satirised by Bemelmans; the inn and hotel have a constant attraction for the writer. Nearly every well-known hotel has at least one book about it, often more; there are nearly a dozen about the Savoy. There have been biographies about famous hoteliers—two at least of César Ritz and two of Sam Shepheard and autobiographies as well—John Fothergill's for example.

There are at least two books about nothing but English inn signs. With all this interest in the subject it is astonishing to find that nobody has ever written a history of the growth of hotels generally.

This is what I set out to do and the subject proved to be quite fascinating. From the very lowest beginnings with mine host virtually an outlaw the hostelry has developed until now the great hotels—Claridges for instance—see nothing unusual in accommodating two or more reigning monarchs (incognito) at the one time. Indeed their Public Relations office appears to function mainly to avoid publicity for their guests. This is not without significance for it often appears that what is now the ultimate in the great hotels is not what is included but what is left out.

César Ritz, for instance, thought that a lounge lowered the tone of a hotel and so the Paris Ritz does not have one, although it does have a famous bar. Claridges on the other hand has a lounge but no bar at all which is perhaps unique in the world of luxury hotels. (It has no cabaret either.)

How has it come about that the vermin-infested caravanserais have developed to the stage where a bar or a lounge lowers their tone?

CHAPTER I

ALMOST THE OLDEST PROFESSION

> ... loveth the stranger, in giving him food and raiment, Love ye
> therefore the stranger; for ye were strangers in the land of Egypt.
>
> Deuteronomy x.18

> Ye shall not eat of anything that dieth of itself; thou mayest give
> it unto the stranger that is within thy gates, that he may eat it ...
>
> Deuteronomy xiv.21

In the earliest records the same words are used for inns and
brothels and no distinction appears to have been drawn between
them. Hence the doubts, to this day, about Rahab, that early
fifth columnist in the reconnaissance Joshua carried out before
using his military band to blast open Jericho's defences.

He "sent out of Shittim two men to spy secretly, saying, Go
view the land, even Jericho. And they went, and came into an
harlot's house, named Rahab, and lodged there."

Generations of young Sunday school teachers have stumbled
over this passage but really we know nothing of Rahab's morals
—only that she kept a lodging-house: two thousand years ago it
was not considered necessary to know more.

(Incidentally, we are told that her house was upon the town
wall. It was because of this that the two spies were able to escape
out of the city. So when the walls of Jericho fell why did not
Rahab's house fall too?)

Rahab is the first landlady we know by name. Where or when
the first inn actually functioned will never be known, any more
than we can ever know when the first men crept out of caves
and started to build their own dwellings.

About 9,000 years ago a village, Jarmo, was settled in Mesopotamia and this is one of the earliest villages so far excavated.
At other places along the Tigris and the Euphrates men started
to make houses of pressed mud bricks with reeds on the mud
floor, to raise crops and to breed animals instead of hunting
them. Slowly these settlements became villages, then cities and
eventually the first Babylonian dynasty was established.

Three codes of law have been found in this area and interpreted, the most important and complete being the code of
Hammurabi of around 1700 B.C.

This was a detailed record of the law on three large pieces of
black rock, about 7ft. 6in. high, and was famous throughout
Mesopotamia. It was, in fact, only an elaboration of previous
codes, just as Moses' Ten Commandments, similarly written on
tablets, was a development of Hammurabi's code. We have no
knowledge today of where Moses' tablets might be but we do
have the infinitely older tablets of Hammurabi.*

There were no less than 284 statutes; the first, for example,
providing that if a man charges another with a capital offence
and fails to make out his case, he will himself be executed, which
no doubt reduced pressure of work in the courts.

Half-way through, in the commercial section, is the first
recorded reference to taverns and it is evident these were in the
nature of brothels with the landlady doubling as barmaid and
prostitute.

Clearly, taverns were in poor repute as the natural haunt for
undesirable characters. The Code required the landlady to report
any customers who planned crimes in her tavern and the penalty
for not doing so was death.

The drinks sold were barley beer and palm-wine. Grape wine
also appears to have been imported from the Lebanon. The
Code sets out the official prices (in other sections it sets out

*Thousands of years ago an Elamite king invaded Babylon, captured the
steles and carried them back to his stronghold, Susa. Through the ages this
town sank under the dust, but at the beginning of this century it was discovered again. When it was excavated the steles were found in fair condition
and are now in the Louvre. If Moses' stele with the Ten Commandments
was found now, archaeologically, it could only be a postscript.

wages and pensions equally dogmatically). Payment for drink had to be made in kind although currency was being used then. It is not possible, therefore, to gauge accurately the cost of a drink then: the regulation sets the price of one type of cheap liquor as six measures of liquor for five similar measures of corn. We know from other records that no less than fifty measures of this liquor could be brewed from five measures of corn. Our earliest records thus show the innkeeper as disreputable, but enjoying a wide profit margin.

On the other hand, if she gave a false measure or watered down her beer the penalty was death, appropriately by drowning.

Although other women frequented the taverns as the men did, high-priestesses (who were regarded as being in indissoluble union with God) were absolutely barred. If one attempted to enter a tavern the penalty was death by burning, this being considered the most effective way of cleansing such defilement of her consecrated body.

The first inns we can trace could hardly have been regarded more unfavourably. Nevertheless, as trade and travel developed some sort of overnight accommodation was required. A load of silk often took up to three years to travel by pack animals from China to Europe. Merchants setting out with their laden caravans for a journey lasting a total of five or six years must have known various points where they could wait, in the winter, for example, for bad weather to improve.

Herman Scriber in his *The History of Roads* mentions a great road system built up in China in the year 2300 B.C. In Europe we have evidence of roads, although not a great system, dating back to 4000 BC. The flint implements of the Danish Ertboll culture of that era were taken to Norway and into the heart of Germany.

Later in the third millennium B.C. amber was greatly prized around the Mediterranean. It was not as dear or difficult to obtain as gold, but a craftsman could display as great a skill with the resin. An amber statuette was worth as much as a good slave. The Etruscans travelled from Italy to the shores of the North Sea and the Baltic trading for amber and four main routes "The amber roads" became established. The evidence now lies in the many wayside graves of these early traders and to a lesser extent by place names—the river Euphrates, for example, is based on the old Persian word "Poretus" meaning bridge and Euphrates means "well bridged"—an important matter to a man on foot or with laden camels.

Rulers of the various areas through which these trade routes passed often encouraged the traffic for the taxes they could levy on the merchandise carried.

They would order space to be made beside suitable water holes for the caravans to rest and later khans were built there. These khans were not inns; they were a cross between a stable, a warehouse and a fortress.

Bands of brigands were a constant threat to any traveller at that time. Runaway slaves and starving peasants joined with condemned criminals to raid and loot with little fear of any official reprisal.

It was essential, therefore, that the merchants travelled together for mutual protection—a convoy system. Even so it often happened then that bandits would attack them at night and so the need grew, lacking suitable caves, for a stout khan.

In his book *Chaldea*, Loftus describes a khan on the road from Baghdad to Babylon and there seems no reason for the pattern of this to have changed in the thousands of years since the wanderings of Isaac and Jacob.

"It is a long and substantial building", wrote Loftus, "in the distance resembling a fortress, being surrounded with a lofty wall and flanked by round towers to defend the inmates in case of attack. Passing through a strong gateway, the guest enters a large court, the sides of which are divided into numerous compartments, open in front, for the accommodation of separate parties and for the reception of goods. In the centre is a spacious raised platform, used for sleeping upon at night or for devotions of the faithful during the day. Between the outer wall and the compartments are wide, vaulted arcades, extending round the entire building, where the beasts of burden are placed. Upon the roof of the arcade is an excellent terrace and over the gateway an elevated tower containing two rooms one of which is open at the sides, permitting the occupants to enjoy every breath of air that passes over the heated plains. The terrace is tolerably clean, but the court and stabling below are ankle deep in chopped straw and filth."

Crowded, stinking and above all noisy (the vermin we take for granted) these khans were scattered along all the great highways of the ancient world and still exist, some seemingly unaltered, in Asia to this day. However, they are hardly what we think of as inns.

The first direct written reference to an inn—apart from the statutes—is in Aristophanes play, *The Frogs*. Dionysus asks Heracles the best route to Hades. "Tell me in case I need them the names of those who befriended you when you went down there after Cerberus; give me a list of them—not to mention the best harbours, bakers, shops, brothels, lodging houses . . . turn-ins and the landladies who had fewest bugs on the premises." It is not just chance that this first written reference to inns mentions bugs. Right down through the centuries until our own period any history of inns could be a history of lice, fleas and bugs.

This is a disagreeable subject and it would be well to dispose of it once and for all now. There were three ways of dealing with vermin.

First and very attractive for those with the right disposition is what we might call the Naval Method. In 1668 Samuel Pepys was travelling with his wife and some friends from Salisbury to Bath. They "went over the smooth plain indeed till night; and then by a happy mistake, and that looked like an adventure, we were carried out of our way to a town where we could lie, since we could not go as far as we would. And there with great difficulty came about ten at night to a little inn, where we were fain to go into a room where a pedlar was in bed, and made him rise; and there wife and I lay, and in truckle-bed Betty Turner and Willett. But good beds, and the master of the house a sober, understanding man . . . By and by to bed, glad of this mistake, because, as it seems, had we gone on as we intended, we could not have passed with our coach and must have lain on the Plain all night . . . 12th (Friday) Up, finding our beds good but lousy, which made us merry. We set out. . . ."

Just that, lousy beds made them merry. No explanation or elaboration; only a flat statement. One wonders if it might have been Pepys, then Secretary to the Admiralty, who coined the old navy jibe "if you can't take a joke you shouldn't have joined".

Another bug course for those without such a developed sense of humour is the Poetic Method. Marcel Schwob in his *The Hostelry* quotes this poet of long ago.

"Hostelry, overrun with vermin, the poet, bitten till deplete of blood, salutes thee . . . For, since thus he might not sleep, he sought to breathe the white moon light through an opening in the wall; and from thence he saw the vendor of women who came knocking at the door very late at night. The merchant called: 'Child! child!'—but the slave was snoring face downward, and with outstretched arms muffled his ears with the coverings. Then the poet wrapped himself in a yellow robe, of the same shade as nuptial veils: this crocus-tinted robe had been left in his possession one morning when a young love-maiden deserted him, clad in a new lover's robe. So the poet, with the outward seeming of a servant, opened the door: and the vendor of women ushered in a numerous band. The breasts of the young girl who entered last were firm as the quince fruit, she was worth at least twenty minae.

" 'Oh servant,' said she, 'I am weary; where is my bed?' 'Oh my dear lady,' said the poet, 'thy friends already occupy every bed in the inn; only the servant's cot is left, if you wish to lie thereon you are welcome.'

"The miserable wretch who cared for all these fair young girls flared the light of the great charred lamp wick in the face of the poet; perceiving a maid servant, neither too beautiful nor well arrayed, he uttered no word of dissent.

"Hostelry, the poet, bitten till deplete of blood thanks thee. The woman who rested with the maid-servant this night was softer than eiderdown, and her fragrant throat was like a perfected fruit. But all this had remained untold, O hostelry, but for the noisy prating of thy cot. The poet fears that the little pigs of Megara may have thus learned of his adventure. O ye who listen to these words, if the 'coi, coi' of these little pigs from Agora to Athenae falsely relates that our poet indulges in low amours come to the hostelry and see his little friend whose love he knew—she whose breasts are as firm as the quince fruit—this poet bitten by the blessed vermin on a moonlit night."

Finally, for those of us living where you never see a woman-vendor from one week to the next (in fact how often do you see a quince about nowadays?) there is the Clerical Method.

The good Parson Woodford describes this in his *Diary of a Country Parson*, when in May, 1783 with his niece Nancy he "... drove to the *Bell Sauvage* in Ludgate Hill and there dined supped and slept ... and was bit terribly by bugs". Nevertheless, he stayed on there and indeed whenever he went back to London on later visits he not only stayed there but strongly recommended the place to all his friends. The bugs got so bad in 1786 that he was obliged to sit up all night. It seems quite clear from his Diary that he regarded even this discomfort as a matter of course, but then every traveller through the centuries took vermin as a matter of course and so shall we.

Almost without exception, almost everywhere, from the earliest records to the very recent past, accommodation overnight on a commercial (or, for that matter, penal) basis connotes bugs, lice and fleas. Let us take it for granted, as the good parson did, and refer to it no more.

Apart from providing a place for travellers to sleep, an inn should provide good cheer and relaxation for the local residents as well as the visitor. It is hard for us, in these days of radio and television to imagine what life must have been like before the days even of the newspaper.

Every community had to have some focal point where people could gather to discuss and to pass on news and rumour. A popular place* was the smithy because of the warmth in winter.

---

*The barber's shop was another centre of gossip, although this was not always sought, any more than it is today. Plutarch tells of a chatty hair-smith of centuries ago asking "How shall I shave you?" and the customer replying "Without speaking."

In Homer's *Odyssey* we have Melantho nagging at an unwelcome guest.

> And you will not go sleep in the smithy
> Nor yet in the club-room, but here you prate.

No doubt wine-sellers' booths would also develop into common meeting places. A great leap forward in inn life then appears to have been made by the Egyptians. They were the first to brew beer. They did not have the abundance of vines, common around most of the Mediterranean and so it was not surprising that they discovered a grain drink.

They also had wine of every sort, palm brandy and a variety of heavily spiced and scented liquors were sold. In fact, not to put too fine a point on it the Egyptians were a drunken lot by Grecian standards and the Greeks took it for granted that the steps of their glorious Parthenon would normally be littered with drunks sleeping it off.

"But remarkable above everything else," writes the Greek geographer Strabo, "is the multitude of persons who resort to the public festivals, and come from Alexandria by the canal. By day and night there are crowds of men and women in boats, singing and dancing without restraint, and with utmost licentiousness. Others, at Canopus itself, keep hostelries, situated on the banks of the canal, which are well adapted for such kinds of diversions and revelry."

This is not the sour comment of an old prude as we see from the bas reliefs on Egyptian tomb decorations and frescoes with banquet pictures of women vomiting and slaves carrying home their unconscious masters.

Juvenal writes bitterly of a drunken brawl and jibes that backward as the Egyptians might appear (then!) their barbarous rabble was advanced as any nation in sensual indulgence.

It may have been the Egyptians who first had the basic idea of an inn—a hostelry serving drink where one can sleep the night. In the tomb of Ranni at El-Keb is depicted a funeral meal with a visitor being pressed to drink and he replies that he will "drink till I am happy, and the mat under me is a good straw bed upon which I can sleep myself sober".

That perhaps is how people started to sleep in inns, and as any women working in an inn—and probably most of those visiting it —were whores this would also develop the trend to provide sleeping accommodation.

Born thus out of drunkenness and harlotry it is hardly surprising that inns and innkeepers were held in such poor repute through the centuries.

Not only did these physical aspects arouse contempt, but until very recent times the view has persisted, perhaps still persists, that the innkeeper himself has prostituted hospitality. In the early days of our ancient civilizations the right of a weary traveller to a night's free shelter and food was taken absolutely for granted. This is still the case among primitive peoples today and it may be that these are inborn traits of humanity going back to the dawn of time and that without such customs mankind itself might not have survived.

Gavin Maxwell makes the point in his *A Reed Shaken by the Wind* which describes his travels in a marshy waste land in Iraq.

He stayed each night in a mudhif, the guest house of a sheikh. These mudhifs are made of reeds like all the other dwellings on the marshes and have no furniture. Servants place rugs and cushions on the floor when a guest arrives and gradually all the men of the village drop in to spend the evening with the visitor.

"Throughout our journey I was struck by the boorishness of Western hospitality by contrast with that of the Arabs. If a stranger rings a doorbell in Europe, he must produce some very good reasons before he can get into the house at all, much less eat there as a guest; yet in the lands where there are neither door nor doorbells the stranger is not asked the reason for his presence, and to hesitate in setting food before him would be shameful. In the parable of the Good Samaritan it is possible that the significance of the travellers passing by on the other side is that they passed, as though quite unaware of the thieves' victim, because had they acknowledged the other's presence at all there would have been no alternative to the actions of the Samaritan.

"Both the Europeans' boorishness and the Arab's hospitality may be no more than separate manifestations of the will to power, but the first must mean security only for the individual, the second for the race."

Nothing could be more unlike these marshlands than the desert wastes of the Middle East, but here the same tradition persists. Alexander Dumas gave an account of Arab life and this was an aspect that impressed him.

"A traveller arrives at a Douait, literally a ring of tents, taking care to strike his spurs noisily against his stirrups to warn the women to keep out of sight. When the owner of a tent hears this signal and comes out, the stranger approaches him, saying 'Dif-erbi—a guest sent by Allah'. ' 'Marhaba-bik' is the reply meaning such a guest is welcome. The host assists him to dismount, takes him into the tent, spreads a rug for him to lie upon and makes sure his horse is well cared for. Whether the stranger is rich or poor he need have no fear for his weapon or his other possessions. Everything will be safe and will be handed to him intact when he leaves. A meal is set before him and the host calls in his neighbours to help entertain the guest, but at the first sign of weariness they all depart leaving the stranger to sleep in peace. If, when morning comes, he wishes to stay longer, he will still be welcome, but if he must go his horse will be saddled and waiting for him. He mounts and says 'May God requite you' and rides away. No one has enquired his name or where he is going, and his host is fully recompensed by word of thanks."

Always it seems that the harder the physical conditions, the greater the obligation of hospitality. Possibly the one place where it is harder to sustain life than in the arid wastes of the desert is the other extreme: the icy wastes of the Arctic. Here hospitality is proffered just as readily and without the need to warn off the women folk. The reverse in fact. As K. A. J. Birket-Smith writes in *The Eskimos*.

"Aleutian good manners even required that the men should place their wives at the disposal of their guests, a circumstance of which the Russian fur hunters were not slow in taking advantage and returned by spreading venereal diseases among the

people. Furthermore, it is everywhere a common custom to exchange wives for a long or short period, and the husbands in these
cases are so far from being jealous of one another that the
exchange of wives is, on the contrary, considered to be one of
the most effective means of emphasizing and strengthening
a friendship. In former days the Greenlanders had a custom
called 'the game of putting out the lamps', and in large communal houses they used to give their visitors an opportunity of
taking part in this evening entertainment.

"It would be a great mistake, however, to see merely licentiousness and vice in these customs. Purely practical circumstances
are often of importance. For instance, a man is going on a long
journey and cannot do without female help for sewing and other
tasks; if his wife is prevented from going with him, owing to
sickness or pregnancy, he makes a temporary exchange with a
friend, whose wife may perhaps want to visit her parents who live
at some distance. In fact, however strange the effect upon us,
that which a superficial application of European moral standards
will condemn is in some cases the highest social duty."

Hospitality was often not only a social duty, it might also be a
religious one. There are repeated instructions to the Jews—in
Deuteronomy already quoted and, for example, in Exodus.

"A stranger shalt thou not wrong, neither shalt thou oppress
him: for ye were strangers in the Land of Egypt . . . If thou
afflict them in any wise and they cry at all unto me, I will surely
hear their cry; and my wrath shall wax hot, and I will kill you
with the sword and your wives shall be widows and your children
fatherless. . . ."

Nevertheless, in time the Jews came to regard the demands of
hospitality binding only if the traveller was also Jewish, perhaps
because of their strict dietary laws. Strangers of other nations
were generally provided an open place where they could pitch
their tents (much as the tourist of today can park his caravan in
the centre square of little French towns and villages).

Greeks, however, knew no such distinction and, at least in the
Heroic age, Greeks above all could claim to be the most generous
of hosts. Even to this day the Greeks have the same word,

Ksenos both for guest and for stranger. Over and over again in the *Odyssey* wayfarers are hustled into strange houses, bathed and anointed with oil and fed sumptuously before they get a chance to identify themselves.

"... (Telemachus) beheld Athene and he went straight to the outer door: for in his heart he counted it shame that a stranger should stand long at the gates ... 'Hail stranger; in our house thou shalt find entertainment, and then, when thou hast tasted food, thou shalt tell of what thou hast need. ...'

"... There Nestor sat with his sons, and around about his people, making ready the feast, were roasting some of the meat and putting forth pieces on spits. But when they saw the strangers they all came thronging about them, and clasped their hands in welcome and bade them sit down ... Meanwhile the fair Polycaste, the youngest daughter of Nestor, bathed Telemachus. And when she had bathed him and anointed him richly with oil, and had cast about him a fair cloak and a tunic, forth from the bath he came. ..."*

Here again we see that the Greeks, like the Arabs, studiously avoided questioning a guest at length until he had been fed and bathed.

Unfortunately, as the glory of Greece started to dim after the Trojan Wars so this unquestioning, open-handed hospitality dies. Perhaps it is a feature of natural progress, mankind was moving on from a primitive, child-like attitude and becoming more discriminating. Now the guest could still expect a warm welcome provided he could first establish his right to hospitality. No problem arose, of course, where the guest and host knew each other. It was when the stranger, a recommended friend or relative of accepted guests, turned up that there might be difficulty.

The solution was the use of hospitality tokens. When a guest

---

*This delightful account of innocent hospitality in the Golden Age so appalled the Liberal Gladstone that he just did not believe it. "It is almost of itself incredible that habitually, among persons of the highest rank and character and without any necessity at all, such things should take place. And, as it is not credible, so neither I think, is it true. The statement that water was poured over (Ulysses) head and shoulders, as he sat in the bath, evidently implies that what may be called essential decency was preserved ...'

left the host broke in two a little token, made of precious metal, ivory or even wood. Each kept a piece which could only be fitted by the other part. Anybody presenting one half at the house of the owner of the other piece would be made welcome. Thus anybody going on a journey would ask around, among friends prepared to recommend him, to see who would lend him suitable tokens. At death they would be bequeathed to somebody considered suitable.

Free hospitality, open or selective, was excellent in unfrequented areas, but inadequate where traffic became heavy. Ships from all the known world were sailing into Athens and inns had to be established to accommodate the foreign sailors. It was the ambition of Xenophon that failing private free hospitality the nation should be the hosts, providing free and clean lodgings for all strangers near every port in Greece. This he wanted to finance from taxes on the goods imported at the various harbours.

Nothing came of this, but hospitality did move on to a national basis with the appointment of *proxenos*. Two Greek cities, or states (they were all small) would each appoint a *proxeno* to the other. The *proxeno* from Corinth to Athens would be responsible for the accommodation of all his fellow Corinthians when they visited Athens. He would appoint guides for them, establish their credit, find them lodgings and "He met every demand which the strangers coming from allied cities could make upon him." It has been suggested that *proxenos* were similar to consuls, but really they were more like the resident couriers employed in foreign holiday resorts by the big travel agencies for the convenience of their clients abroad.

The ordinary inn was also becoming established and eventually became so common throughout Greece that in the drama it was the practice to have an inn entrance incorporated into every stage setting. The stage scene normally had three doors. The centre one might appear to open into a palace or a grotto or whatever the play needed. The door on the left invariably opened into an inn unless the play was a tragedy, in which case the door on the right opened into an inn (and the door on the left then opened into a prison).

It seems to have been in Byzantium that tavern life got its greatest hold. Aelian writes "The Byzantines loved wine so passionately they quitted their houses and rented them to the strangers who came to live in their city, in order that they might establish themselves in taverns. They also left their women to the foreigners and thus committed two crimes at the same time, drunkenness and prostitution . . .* during the siege of Byzantium, Leonidas, their General, seeing the soldiers had abandoned their posts on the walls, which were then being heavily attacked by the enemy, and that they passed their entire days in their accustomed haunts, ordered taverns to be established upon the ramparts. That ingenious artifice held them, although a little late, and they did not again abandon their posts. There was no longer a reason for doing so."

If they could run a war like this, one is not so surprised at the readiness with which the old Greek states took up arms against each other.

By the standards of their times, however (despite what the

---

*Over a thousand years later Marco Polo is to complain of exactly the same practice in another pleasure-loving area thousands of miles away. "When strangers arrive (at Kamul) and desire to have lodging and accommodation at their houses they give positive orders to their wives, daughters, sisters, and other female relations to indulge their guests in every wish, whilst they themselves leave their homes, and retire into the city, and the stranger lives in the house with the females as if they were his wives and they send whatever necessaries may be wanted; but for which, it is to be understood, they expect payment, nor do they return to their houses so long as the strangers remain with them. This abandonment of the females of their family to accidental guests, who assume the same privileges and meet with the same indulgences as if they were their own wives, is regarded by these people as doing them honour and adding to their reputation; considering the hospitable reception of strangers, who (after the perils and fatigues of a long journey) stand in need of relaxation, as an action agreeable to their deities. The women are in truth very handsome, very sensual, and fully disposed to conform in this respect to the injunction of their husbands. It happened at the time when Mangu Khan held his court in this province, that the above scandalous custom coming to his knowledge, he issued an edict strictly commanding the people of Kamul to relinquish a practice so disgraceful to them, and forbidding individuals to offer lodging to strangers, who should be obliged to accommodate themselves at a house of public resort or caravanserai." Eventually, because of this ruling (they said) the crops failed and they persuaded the Khan to repeal his edict "to the great delight of all the people who, to the present day, observe their ancient practice".

Romans said), Greeks generally were far from being drunkards
and, indeed, a "Greek hangover" meant to waken with a clear
head and feeling well. One of the reasons was that it was unusual
to drink wine undiluted. Generally it was mixed with water and
the original cocktail-bar kings were the slaves who could mix a
warm wine with cool water to produce a beverage "gracious to
the palate in taste and in temperature". Indeed there were establishments called *thermopolia* where nothing but hot water was
served, sometimes with infusions of suitable plants, like our
present day tea.

With acceptance of the inn came government control and three
inspectors of wine (*oenoptae*) were appointed in Athens to see
that the innkeepers obeyed the various laws regulating drink
sales and taxes. However, they were concerned only with the
drink regulations and perhaps spying on behalf of the government. The quality of an inn as such did not concern them.

It was not only Xenophon who felt that this was not good
enough. Plato also expressed strong views in his Laws.

He was appalled by the general greed for money so that "all
the lines of life connected with the retail trade, commerce, inn-
keeping, have fallen under suspicion and become utterly disreputable. For if what I trust may never be and will not be, we were
to compel, if I may say a ridiculous thing, the best men everywhere to keep taverns for a time or carry on retail trade, or do
anything of that sort; or if, in consequence of some fate or necessity, the best women were compelled to follow similar callings,
then we should know how agreeable and pleasant all these things
are: and if all such occupations were managed on incorrupt principles, they would be honoured as we honour a mother or a
nurse. For the sake of trade, a man opens lodgings in a lonely
place, a long way from anywhere. He receives bewildered
travellers in barely tolerable quarters, or affords warmth, quiet
and rest in his close rooms to people driven in by angry storms.
And then after receiving them as friends he does not provide
them with hospitable entertainment according to that reception,
but holds them to ransom like captive enemies whom he has got
into his clutches, on the most exorbitant, unjust rascally terms.

It is these offences and others like them, shamefully common in all such callings, which have brought discredit upon all ministration to men's needs."

Xenophon and before him Herodotus not only failed to bring back the great days of the open hospitality of the Heroic age, but neither had they ever been able to interest their countrymen in establishing a posting service in Greece, such as Darius had in Persia. Herodotus had seen the Persian Royal Road which, in fact, had its origin long before the Persian Empire. It was about eighteen hundred miles long and connected Sardis (where King Croesus made his celebrated pile by utilizing a new method of refining gold) with Susa, near the Persian Gulf, where Darius the First built a palace fit for a King of Kings.

Herodotus was born about 484 B.C. and he had been greatly impressed by the Persian system.

"52. Now the nature of the road is as I shall show. All along it are the king's stages and exceeding good hostelries, and the whole of it passes through country that is inhabited and safe." He then details the journey, the river crossings, often ferries guarded by fortresses and concludes . . .

"53. Thus the whole tale of stages is an hundred and eleven. So many resting-places then there are in the going up from Sardis to Susa . . . and if each day's journey be an hundred and fifty furlongs, then the sum of the days spent is ninety, neither more nor less."

Although the journey took the ordinary traveller three months, there is evidence that the king's messengers could travel it in a week and Herodotus describes the speed with which Xerxes sent news of his disastrous sea-battle. ". . . as many days as there are in the whole journey, so many are the men and horses that stand along the road, each horse and man at the interval of a day's journey; and these are stayed neither by snow nor rain nor heat nor darkness from accomplishing their appointed course with all speed. The first rider delivers his charge to the second, the second to the third and thence it passes on from hand to hand, even as in the Greek torch-bearers race in honour of Hephaestus."

Presumably the Greeks were not interested in such a posting

system because their population was not spread out over a vast territory as the Persian Empire covered. The little Greek states and cities were too close together for the system really to attract them (even if they had made peace for long enough to work together on such a project). Sea travel in any case was an easy method of communication for them.

The Romans, however, were quick to see that to hold their great Empire together some such system was essential and it is with the arrival of the Roman Republic that we start to see good posting houses and inns across the great routes of the ancient world.

CHAPTER 2

WHEN IN ROME

Such persons [female inn staff] shall be held as being immune against the judicial proceedings of the law against adultery and prostitution as the very indignity of their life is an insult to the laws they should observe.

Theodosius

FOR over a thousand years the Romans governed practically all the civilized world and a very large part of it for most of another thousand years. To do this they had to have good communications.

It is hard for us, in these days of telephones and regular postal services to imagine life where no man's voice carried further than he could shout and every message had to be conveyed by couriers on foot or horseback. If speed mattered, and it did, the Romans had to have the best possible road and posting system. They had. Nothing like their road lay-out had ever existed before nor have we yet achieved its like again.

When the power of the Empire was at its height a citizen could leave Hadrian's Wall, in the North of England, and travel on first-class roads for four thousand five hundred miles to Ethiopia. He could make a round trip from Egypt through Carthage to Spain, France and London and then go back through Cologne, Italy, Greece and Damascus. He would cover over ten thousand miles without ever having to think about currency problems or visas and on first-class roads all the time. Where can we do that today? North America perhaps?

The Western world still has ample evidence of Roman building skill. In Segovia, for example, their aqueduct, over half a mile long and much of it over one hundred feet high, was built without any mortar at all, so well were the stones made to fit together. It still carries water today as it did when Trajan built it almost two thousand years ago.

In North Africa there is a memorial altar on which an architect, Nomius Datus, inscribed his account of building a tunnel at Saldae. There had been trouble while he had been away from the site and he was blamed on his return.

"What more could I have done? I began by demarcating the outlying spurs of the mountain and traced on the mountain ridge the line of the tunnel as precisely as possible. I drew plans and cross-sections of the whole work and handed them to the governor of Mauretania. I even took the precaution of summoning the foreman and his workmen and in their presence, with the help of two shifts of experienced men, I began ... the excavation. What more could I have done? But during the four years I was absent ... the foreman and his assistants had committed one mistake after the other; both the galleries of the tunnel had diverged from the straight, both to the right, and had I arrived a little later, Saldae would have possessed two tunnels instead of one."

Tunnels that were chopped out of solid rock at a foot or two a month, because the Romans would rather go through a mountain than around it.

When we see the quality of their roads and bridges we can imagine that they built posting houses of similar quality, but little of these now stands.

Lanciani has described the remains of the Roman Mansio which has been excavated in the Great St. Bernard.

"The Roman hospice (mansio in summo Paenini) stood a quarter of a mile to the south of the present one and comprised a temple to the god of the mountain, a hospice for travellers, stables and watering troughs, and store houses for fuel and provisions. The mansio or hospice was built of stone with an elaborate system of hypocausts and flues for the distribution of heat through the guest rooms. The roof made of tiles from the lime kilns of the Val d'Aosta, had projecting eaves in the old Swiss style."

These superb posting houses stood on all the main roads generally in a town or village. In between at distances of five to eight miles were about half a dozen *mutations*. These were usually just stables where the horses could be changed but without any other facility unless an inn were erected privately nearby.

Primarily this system existed to provide a postal service for the government but there was also travelling accommodation for the select few. These were officials and couriers of the Roman government and not the general public. A travelling consul or prefect wanted to know that he could sleep safely at night. If access to a hospice were freely available to any traveller how could officials of higher rank feel safe, particularly when they were travelling through conquered territories, hostile to Rome?

Only those, therefore, bearing a "diplomata tractatorium" could use the posting services. These documents were issued to suitably qualified Romans, usually travelling on government business.

We have a specimen of the form that would be completed for an ambassador taking up a foreign post.

TO ALL OUR OFFICIALS AT THEIR POSTS OF DUTY

Greeting:

Know ye that we have delegated . . . an illustrious gentleman, to be our legate or ambassador to . . . We, therefore, command you by these presents to aid his excellency, to provide and furnish his excellency with . . . horse, to collect such quantity of supplies as to him shall seem good and reasonable, in places proper and convenient; furnish . . . ordinary sumpter horses and . . . in addition; . . . bread; . . . hogsheads of wine; . . . cattle; . . . hogs; . . . suckling pigs; . . . sheep; . . . lambs; . . . geese; . . . pheasants; . . . chickens; . . . oil; . . . of pickle; . . . of honey; . . . of vinegar; . . . of cummin; . . . of pepper; . . . of coste; . . . of cloves; . . . of aspic; . . . of cinnamon; . . . grains of mastic; . . . dates; . . . pistache; . . . almonds; . . . wax; . . . of salt; . . . of oils; . . . ricks of hay; . . . of oats; and . . . of straw.

TREETOPS HOTEL *An annexe of the Outspan Hotel in Myeri at the foot of Mount Kenya. An artificial moon provides permanent lighting and salt licks have been attracting every sort of wild animal for years. A young lady spent a night here in February 1952 and breakfasted, unaware that her father had died and she was Queen of England. This hotel was burned down by Mau Mau but a bigger structure has replaced it.*

MONSERRAT MONASTERY *in Spain on the Montserrat (Montsagrat —sacred mountain) where medieval legend located the Holy Grail. The monastery was founded in 880 and still today offers traditional austere hospitality to the pilgrims, as most monasteries once did.*

Look ye that all these things are furnished him in full and entirely, in a place convenient, and let everything be accomplished without delay.

This is good for one journey only and generous provision is made for normal stores as the ambassador would be travelling with all his household, slaves, etc.

Regular government travellers would obtain a document good for the lifetime of the official who signed it. At first these were very hard to obtain and a traveller, no matter how important or urgent his mission, had no authority without one.

Inevitably, however, there was some abuse of the system and people with friends in the right quarters were able to secure passes to which they were not entitled. One imagines they must have been the ultimate status symbol of all time. In effect the bearer was granting everybody along his route the privilege of supplying his party with anything they might need in the way of horses, food or shelter. If there were any shortage at the posting station then a levy was made on the local inhabitants. Any reasonable wish of the traveller with a *diplomata tractatorium* had the weight of imperial sanction.

Coveted even more in the days of the Republic was a *libera legatio*—a pass issued as a special favour to a distinguished elder. This gave all the advantages of the *diplomata* without any obligation at all. Abuses of the privilege caused constant criticism.

Life was not always so lush, particularly in the early days of the Republic. Plutarch tells us "For the most part Caesar slept in his chariot or in litters so that he could still be active even when resting . . . He travelled with such speed that he needed no more than eight days to reach the Rhone from Rome."

When there were no posting houses the rich traveller who was not in such a hurry would have tents erected by the way. Generally they were travelling in climates that were warm and with a retinue of slaves to carry every luxury, so this provided far better accommodation than any wayside inn. We will consider this "camping" practice in more detail later. For the time being it is enough to say that there was no hardship involved—when

Tiberius travelled he had complete portable garden plots to accompany him, with growing melons and early vegetables. Camping out he may have been, but he was not roughing it.

It was the traveller staying at inns who had to rough it. These inns—*tabernae** or *cauponae*—lined all the highways and varied from the filthiest little wine booths to more substantial establishments. Frequently great estate owners would set up *cauponae* on the edge of their estates, if only to provide themselves with some refreshment on their own travels. A slave would be installed to manage the inn and he would endeavour to make a profit by selling wine and food stolen from the estate.

Nearer the cities and in them the inns and taverns were run by freedmen, very frequently Syrians and other Levantines "nations born for slavery" as Cicero puts it so nicely. Occasionally a retired gladiator would invest his savings in just the same way that our retired footballers, boxers and the like set up as mine host today. There were even inn signs "Ad Galum"—at the Sign of the Cock or "Ad Rotam"—The Wheel.

The Roman appetite for food or drink in the later centuries was far more gross than that of the Greeks, but in the early days of the Republic they were generally temperate. They had a phrase—to drink like a Greek—which meant to get stinking drunk and normally the early Romans at least drank water with their wine.

> In an inn at Ravenna the other day
> I was bilked by the wiles of a cheat
> When I ordered my wine mixed with water
> the gay deceiver retailed me wine neat

wrote Martial sarcastically.

How the travellers fared might well depend on the fertility of the surrounding country, as much as anything else. Polybius, travelling in Southern Italy, gives the first account we have of catering on what was later to be known as the American plan.

---

*The English word *tavern* is derived from this of course, but originally *taberna* merely meant a shop and had to be described—thus around the Forum were the *tabernae argentariae*—the shops of the bankers. It is perhaps of interest that in parts of Scotland, particularly Glasgow, taverns nowadays are often referred to as *shops*.

". . . the cheapness and abundance of all articles of food will be most clearly understood from the following facts: travellers in this country, who put up in inns, do not bargain for each separate article they require, but ask what is the charge per diem for one person. The inn-keepers, as a rule, agree to receive guests providing them with enough of all they require for half an as per diem, i.e. the fourth part of an obol, the charge being very seldom higher." (An obol, at that time, would buy about two and a half gallons of wheat.)

It is particularly interesting to have this account because centuries later staying in hotels in the same area Norman Douglas found exactly the opposite practice.

"It is customary here not to live en pension or pay a fixed price for any meal, the smallest item, down to a piece of bread, being conscientiously marked against you. My system, elaborated after considerable experimentation, is to call for this bill every morning and for the first day or two after arrival, dispute in friendly fashion every item, cutting down some of them. Not that they overcharged; their honesty is notorious, and no difference is made in this respect between a foreigner and a native. It is a matter of principles . . . it is your duty to show above all things that you are not a Scemo—witless, soft-headed—the unforgiveable sin in the south. You may be a forger or cut-throat—why not? It is a vocation like any other, a vocation for *Men*. But whoever cannot take care of himself, i.e. of his money—is not to be trusted in any way of life: he is of no account: he is no man . . .

"Of course the inns are often dirty, and not only in their sleeping accommodation. The reason is that, like Turks or Jews, their owners do not see dirt (there is no word for dirt in the Hebrew language) they think it is odd when you draw their attention to it."

At least, not everything has changed. The first, and so far as I know, the only hotel bill that has ever been inscribed in stone notes much higher prices.

A relief was found at Aesernia (it is now in Paris) which can be translated as:

"Erected in his life time by C. Calidus Eroticus to himself and Fannie Voluptas. Innkeeper my bill, please. You have got down: a pint of wine, one as: bread one as: food, two asses. Agreed. Girl, eight asses. Agreed. Hay for mule, two asses. That mule is going to make me bankrupt."

The Romans, as the Greeks before them, always accepted that women connected with the *cauponae* or *tabernae* were whores. When various laws forbidding adultery were passed from time to time inn women were always specifically excluded as beyond the pale. Further, the laws which forbade certain classes of female slaves from being sold into prostitution equally forbade their being sold to inn-keepers.

The inn-keepers themselves were similarly below the law. They were not admitted to military service, they could not normally bring a legal action in court, they could not take the oath and they could not act as guardians for children. In short neither mine host nor his lady were held in high regard.

On 24th August in A.D. 79 Pliny the Elder was at Misenum where he commanded the Roman fleet. There was a report that Vesuvius was erupting and he took the fleet over to see if the inhabitants of the neighbouring towns needed help. By the time the eruption was finished Herculaneum lay under a layer of ashes sixty-five feet deep, nearby Pompeii was under twenty foot and Pliny was dead.

This tragedy has preserved for us, under an almost perfect shell of natural mortar, life as it stopped that August afternoon. One building is a typical inn as we read of them at that time.

The wall of one room is decorated by four paintings. The first is of a customer fondling a wench who is resisting him and under is the legend Nolo Cum Myrtal (I don't want to go with Myrtle). The next shows three women drinking.

The third is of two men gambling with counters and dice; they are starting to argue. The final scene shows them brawling and being ejected by the landlord.

A typical cross-section of tavern life it seems and not one to attract the respectable or fastidious. The ordinary traveller could not afford to be too fastidious and we get a fair idea from old

Spanish *posadas* and *fondas* of what many of the better Roman inns would have been like. In her brilliant book, *Two Middle Aged Ladies in Andalucia*, Penelope Chetwode describes travel on horseback in remote Spanish villages.

"The *posada* is an inn with stables attached, the animals being often better housed and better fed than the human beings. Both enter by the same front door, which in the smaller *posadas* leads directly into the living-room. Your horse is lead through this into the great cavernous stables beyond, which are cool in summer and warm in winter. In the larger *posadas* there are big double doors, open during the day which lead into a covered cobbled yard where the muleteers and donkey boys sleep on straw palliasses. At the far end are stables with rows of mangers, sometimes over a hundred, all along the walls with pegs above them . . . On either side of the cobbled yard are the kitchen and dining room and stairs leading up to the bedroom . . . At least one of these bedrooms is used as a store for barley, maize, almonds, pumpkins and pomegranates. There is seldom any glass in the windows. Ill-fitting and dilapidated wooden shutters keep out some of the draughts and all of the light, a feeble artificial variety of which is provided by a 15-watt bulb usually hung over the foot of your bed.

"The *posada* often has the advantage over the *fonda* in that it possesses only stable sanitation. When the water variety is attempted it is always a dismal failure, partly because there is never any water laid on. You simply ladle it into the pan from a large stone jar, and the stink from the drains is overpowering. The Spaniards possess a great variety of talents but plumbing is not one of them.

"The technique of using stable sanitation successfully and without undue strain on the nerves is as follows: when you want to enter the stable to attend to your horse, you open the door with a smile on your face, switch on the light and advance towards the animal, welcoming any help from your landlord or fellow-guest which may be offered. When, however, you wish to enter it for the other purpose you go towards the door with a look of grim determination upon your face, do not turn on the lights, and slam the door hard behind you. Should you hear a giant pee-ing close by it is almost certain to be a mule or donkey; and when your eyes, growing used to the dim light, discern the figure of your landlady squatting in a corner, the custom is for both of you to roar with laughter as if this clandestine meeting were the most natural thing in the world, which indeed it is.

"The menus in *fondas* and *posadas* differ little, but whereas in the former meals are provided, in the latter the traveller can please himself; he can either bring his own food and cook it on the open kitchen fire or he can eat what his landlady sets before him. . . ."

These establishments have certainly altered little since Ford's visit over a century ago and he was of the opinion then that they were still practically the same as they had been in classical times. Any horseman travelling through the Roman Empire could have put up in something little different from Mrs. Chetwode's *posada*.

There may have been some difference, apart from the electric light. Claudius Galenus was an eminent Roman doctor who travelled widely in the second century A.D. He writes convincingly and factually of innkeepers serving up human flesh as pork and cites one case where a landlord and his family were caught actually preparing a human victim for the oven.

One just has a little twinge of doubt because he also tells of a travelling companion who found a human finger in his stew. This hoary old veteran of a story, with such racial derivatives as the curried cat in Chinese restaurants or dog-meat sandwiches for coloured imigrants must have started somewhere. Perhaps Galenus was telling the genuine original story which has been cooked up in so many different ways in the centuries since.

In the cities, the taverns gradually became better. In the early days they were the resort only of slaves and the poorer freedmen, sailors and the like. Standards improved slowly until men-about-town like Horace and Martial write frequently of going into taverns.

Florus, a poet who was a friend of Hadrian, wrote him:

No Caesar would I want to be
Inspecting Britain's wastes
Lurking in savage (Germany)
No Scythian frosts would suit my tastes.

To which Hadrian replied:

No Florus would I want to be
Inspecting bar-maids' waists,
Lurking in a hostelry
No fat round insects suit my tastes.

which might not be great verse or even very witty, but it does show that by then the Emperor could talk even jestingly of a friend lurking in a hostelry.

Other emperors had a much more intimate knowledge of taverns, but these were dissolute roisterers out for amusement at any price.

Julius Capitolinus felt strongly about Verus, who at least had precedents to go on.

"Emulating the examples set by Caligula, Nero and Vitellius he frequented the taverns and haunts of vice at nights, his head enveloped in a cowl such as is worn by vagrant wayfarers; disguised in this manner he mixed with the brawling roisterers and bullies, took part in their battles, and came home with his face and body a mass of bruises. In spite of his disguise, he was well known in these taverns. Sometimes he amused his ennui by throwing heavy pieces of money at the vases and porcelains, to break them."

Not quite what one thinks of as a Roman orgy perhaps and one might even warm to Gallenius who "passed all his nights in the taverns, and lived and amused himself with all the go-between, mimes, actors, actresses and witty rascals", Pollio complained. Sounds fun really, and again one is hard put not to feel sympathy for poor stupid Claudius, unexpectedly transformed from buffoon to Emperor when he was nearly fifty and arousing the bitter scorn of Suetonius.

"Often he shows such heedlessness in word and deed that

one would suppose he did not know or care to whom or with whom or when or where he was speaking. During a debate about butchers and vintners, he cried out in the Senate, 'who can live without a snack, I ask you' and then went on to describe the abundance of the old taverns to which he used to go for wine in earlier days."*

Particularly degenerate sets of the aristocracy might sometimes seek thrills in the squalor of tavern vice, but generally the upper classes resorted to the public baths for their pleasures and orgies. These were open day and night and by the time Caligula came to power nude mixed bathing was accepted practice and wine was freely available—Martial writes of somebody "unable to return home sober from the baths".

Attached to the baths were sumptuous dining-rooms available for parties which could not be accommodated at home. Wedding breakfasts, for example, would usually be enjoyed here and Juvenal writes of young brides celebrating their nuptials under graphic paintings of nudes.

Eventually Sumptuary Laws were passed to restrain the prodigality of these private banquets and the laws applied to meals at home as well as at the *nympheae* (the establishments attached to the baths were so called because the newly married girls were called nymphs). Gates and doors had to be left open to allow the censors to make a rapid inspection and there was a limit on the amount of money that a household could spend on food daily (normally ten asses increased to two hundred on a wedding day) and a daily limit of three pounds of fresh meat.

Like American Prohibition these laws were so unpopular that they could not be enforced for long. The Romans ruled the world and if they could not have an orgy when they wanted one, who could?

---

*It would have been better for poor Claudius had he stuck to his taverns when he might have died a natural death. Instead he accepted the purple to be poisoned later in the most ham-handed fashion on record. Tacitus and Suetonius agree that his ambitious niece-wife Agrippina employed a professional poisoner who made a botch of the job. She simply made the Emperor sick. A doctor was summoned and Agrippina had to make a quick arrangement with him to put a better poison on the end of the feather he was using to tickle the Emperor's throat.

CHAPTER 3

THE THOUSAND YEARS AFTER ROME

Strong beer, a liquor extracted with very little art from wheat or barley and corrupted into a certain semblance of wine, was sufficient for the gross purposes of German debauchery.

Tacitus

THE Roman Empire died slowly. A thousand years was to pass after the legions left Britain before Italian peasants brought their farm carts into mighty Rome for the statues. Rome really was finished when, all else having been looted, these oafs burned the glorious statuary to use the lime for a fertilizer.

However, as far as the Romanized Britons were concerned the fifth century saw the start of the Dark Ages in Europe.

We have evidence of some provision for the traveller before the Romans came; this was apparently under the supervision of the Druids, primarily because visitors were generally travelling to religious shrines. There they would stay in open houses kept by *beatochs*. In Ireland there were *bruighs*, people provided with land and stock to keep beds and stabling for travellers, together with such amusements as backgammon boards.

The Romans had brought, although not immediately, the vine to Britain, but after they left the Saxons came and they cared for nothing but beer. This was made from barley which was so named from beer-lec—beer plant. The Danes refer to it as ale and there has been a suggestion that this has the same derivation as yule, with its connections with yuletide, yule logs, etc.

Ale houses were established generally at road junctions. Inns in Rome were always identified by some foliage, perhaps vine leaves around a pole, or a bush or some leaves to indicate a fresh vintage (hence the saying a good wine needs no bush; i.e. a good inn became well known without advertising). This tradition of a bush on the end of a pole (the ale-stake or the ale-pole) as an inn sign continued in Saxon England and they are in the pictures we have of dreadful old crones welcoming callers to their little one-storey ale-houses. Although we have Saxon workmanship surviving in a few churches no trace remains of these old ale houses, built no doubt of wattle and daub or timber.

The few ancient inns still to be seen with reed and wattle interior walls, like the *Kingsbridge,* near the Cattle Market in Totnes, were built several centuries later.

Some half-a-dozen inns claim to be the oldest in England, but as they were established before any licence was required and records are scant it is impossible to say which is really the oldest. The *Church House Inn* at Rattery in South Devon, for example, dates from 1026, but there are others older still.

A few of the earliest Saxon inns may have accommodated travellers, but there is little direct reference to them. There are a few statutes to ensure good order in the inns—a decree by Ethelbert in 616 and another by Ina, King of Wessex in 730, and King Edgar reduced the number of ale-houses allowing one only to each village.

He also ordered that inside each drinking tankard pegs should be fixed. These peg tankards contained half a gallon and were divided into eight levels by the pegs. The tankard passed from hand to hand and the law forbade anybody to drink more than one peg (half a pint) at a draught.

Eventually, however, it seems that this peg-drinking became competitive (no doubt this is the origin of the phrase "to take him down a peg or two") and Anselm decreed in 1102 "Let no priest go to drinking bouts, nor drink to pegs".

At this stage the inn was more for the drinker than the traveller, but travellers got little encouragement from any quarter. Ina of Wessex, in fact, passed another *doom* (law): "If a man from afar or a stranger travels through a wood off the highway and neither shouts nor blows a horn he shall be assumed a thief and as such may either be slain or put to ransom."

Apart from a few merchants, generally in Saxon times travellers were connected with the Court or the Church. They would not be interested in the primitive accommodation of a wayside inn and either enjoyed private hospitality or erected their own tents. We have Aldred the Provost noting a prayer book "... at Oakley in Wessex on Wednesday, St. Lawrence's Day, for Aelfsige the Bishop in his tent, when the moon was five nights old ..." This was the Bishop of Chester-le-Street who had travelled so far afield to attend a council meeting. Fortunately St. Lawrence's Day is in August.

Again we have an Aelfric bequeathing to his bishop "... my tent and my bedclothing, the best that I have had out on my journey with me ..." and other wills make similar references.

As we see constantly, private hospitality for royalty was as much a trial as an honour. There is a record at this time of a visit by King Athelston. His staff inspected the selected household the day before to confirm that provisions were adequate and found the supply of mead to be short.

Aethelflaed the hostess prayed to the Virgin and as a result (presumably) although the mead flowed freely all day "as is the custom at royal banquets" the supply did not fail.

The first monastery had been built at Canterbury about AD 600 by Augustine and almost at the same time Aidan was introducing Celtic monasticism in the North. These monasteries would have offered hospitality to the wayfarer but unfortunately, they were not designed to last long.

When the Vikings reached Britain in 787 the religious houses, not constructed for defence like the castles, offered rich pickings. Lindisfarne off the Northumberland coast was the first to go and within a hundred years all the monasteries had to be abandoned. Alfred the Great found no monastic life left when he came to the throne and he had to import a foreign community for his foundation at Athelny.

This did not survive and it was not until the Norman invasion that monastery life really flourished in England. The new owners of great estates scattered through England could well afford to make generous grants of land to endow monasteries, abbeys or priories. As a standard practice these all offered the traveller hospitality.

More effective than this in encouraging travel was William's method of distributing his lands. He had seen the dukes of France secure in their great estates defying a weak central authority. He was going to have nothing like that in his new kingdom. The nobles to whom he was indebted were duly rewarded, but with estates strung across the land. As a result of this, for example, when the Earl of Lincoln died in 1240 the Bishop of Lincoln advised his widow how to manage her estates;

"She must at Michaelmas plan out her year's movements, so that she could live economically on the produce of her estates but not impoverish any manor by staying in it too long. Those things which must be bought, such as wine, wax and clothes, could be best bought at the fairs; for the manors in the eastern counties, Boston fair; for the Winchester lands, Southampton fair, and for the west country estates, Bristol fair; for cloth, St. Ives was best."

The King himself also moved about his new country continually and of course where he went his court went with him.

Charlemagne had set the pattern for this a couple of centuries before. He had spent his life journeying through his kingdom with his family and court, staying on one of his own estates until all the food resources were finished or visiting the homes of nobility on his route. Dr. E. Power in her *Medieval People* quotes G. Faigniez to give a vivid picture of exactly what such a visitation might mean.

"There was a certain Bishopric which lay full in Charles's path when he journeyed and which indeed he could hardly avoid: and the Bishop of this place always anxious to give satisfaction put everything that he had at Charles's disposal. But once the Emperor came quite unexpectedly and the Bishop in great anxiety had to fly hither and thither like a swallow and had not only the palaces and houses, but also the courts and squares swept and cleaned and then tired and irritated came to meet him. The most pious Charles noticed this and after examining all the various details he said to the Bishop 'My kind host you always have everything clean for my arrival.' Then the Bishop, as if divinely inspired, bowed his head and grasped the King's never-conquered right hand, and hiding his irritation, kissed it and said 'It is but right, my Lord, that wherever you come all things should be thoroughly cleansed.' Then Charles, of all Kings the wisest, understanding the state of affairs said to him, 'If I empty I can also fill' and he added 'you may have that estate which lies close to your Bishopric and all your successors may have it until the end of time'."

There is no record of William or his successors giving away the odd estate like this. When he arrived at a town for the night his marshal marked the best houses with chalk for the lords and officers of the household to move into and the owners had to make the best of it. The King himself would be in one of his own or a liege's castle or failing that a monastery and sometimes tents were erected. "As a result the baggage train of this roving court was a formidable sight. A long string of pack-horses carried tents, furniture, bedding, cooking utensils, personal luggage, and stocks of food. Even the royal chapel with its relics and its candles carefully guarded by the chaplain, jogged its way along in this royal cavalcade on the backs of a couple of horses. Those who packed and unpacked the train acquired the skilled routine of modern circus hands, but only at a heavy expense of man power were the royal family and the nobles who travelled with the King spared as much personal inconvenience and discomfort as possible. Even for them such journeys made at all times of the year were very exacting; for the scores of servants, whose incessant manual work alone made this type of life possible, there was no comfort and only the briefest pleasures."

These journeys were incessant and we have a record of a later monarch—Edward I in 1299—moving seventy-five times in the year.

"This itinerant court had several disadvantages in addition to the discomfort which constant travelling and living out of saddle-bags imposed upon its members. Its approach terrified townsfolk and countryfolk alike, for one never knew what demands it would make for food supplies, or even for young men and women to enter the royal service. Its unpredictable movements made it difficult for petitioners and messengers to find the King, and, as government tended to become more complicated, it imposed increasing burdens upon the royal officers responsible for administration."

At first even the Royal Treasury accompanied the King, with the Chancellor carrying the chequer-board (a chess board counting device used to show illiterate taxpayers the correctness of additions and subtractions—hence the Chancellor of the Exchequer).

The great lords also travelled with as big a retinue as possible for safety as well as prestige. They could not command accommodation as the King could, but hospitality was usually offered.

When the Normans first travelled in conquered England they were in enemy territory and naturally tried to reach a Norman camp or fortress before nightfall. If any spur were needed this would aid the development of unquestioned hospitality among the Norman barons. They did not regard this as merely a duty however; at a time when there were no newspapers and a lute was about the limit of home entertainment a stranger with fresh stories and perhaps news, was always welcome.

He would eat with his host in the great hall, the lords on the dais and their followers at lower tables at right angles. When they were ready to retire these lower tables were taken out of the hall, fresh rushes and perhaps straw mattresses put down and there the lower orders lay themselves. The house might be large enough to have a guest room for the visitor or he might be invited into his host's bedroom.

Some barons, on main routes, finding they were getting more visitors than was comfortable, built a hostel outside the main hall for the followers of their noble guests. Apart from convenience this reduced the chance of treachery in the middle of the night and became common in later troubled times. This was the first step to the hotel we know today. A further step is described by Larwood in his *English Inn Signs*.

"Coats of arms, crests and badges gradually made their appearance at the doors of shops and inns. The reasons which dictated the choice of such subjects were various—tradition has it that one of the principal was this. In the Middle Ages the houses of the nobility, both in town and country, when the families were absent, were used as hostelries for travellers. The family arms hung in front of the house, and the most conspicuous charge in those arms gave a name to the establishment amongst passers-by. These, unacquainted with the mysteries of heraldry, e.g. called a Lion Gules or Azure by the vernacular name of the Red or Blue Lion. Such coats of arms gradually became popular and inn-keepers began to adopt them, hanging out red lions and green dragons as the best way to acquaint the public that they offered food and shelter. The palace of St. Lawrence Poulteney, the town residence of Charles Brandon, Duke of Suffolk and also the Dukes of Buckingham were called the Rose from that badge being hung up in front of the house. It is referred to in King Henry VIII—Chapter 1 Scene 2."

Most inns, however, would have as a sign the coat of arms of the local lord primarily because it would be standing on his land and perhaps the proprietor would be somebody, a steward or the like, formerly in his employ. The large number of Red Lions throughout the land appear to originate from John O'Gaunt's badge. J. Bickerdyke, in his *Curiosities of Ale and Beer* tells the story which probably accounts for the continued survival.

An old couple had bought an inn and decided that its name should be religious rather than worldly. They summoned the village sign painter:

Landlord: Well, John, me and my missis have been thinking about this sign and we hear as you're up to painting almost anything.

Signpainter (*proudly*): Yes, mister, I can do you pretty well what you like: the Red Lion and so as that.

Landlord: No, John, that ain't quite what we want. Me and my missis have been athinking as we'd like to have the Angel and Trumpet. Now, can you do it?

Signpainter: Well, mister, I can do um: but you'd better by half have the Red Lion: it's a deal thirstier sign.

Landlord (*firmly*): No, John, we must have the Angel and Trumpet so if you can't do un, say so, and we must get some un as can.

Signpainter: All right, I'll paint the Angel and Trumpet, but (*aside*) I specs it'll be a good deal like the Red Lion.

Any poor wayfarer might claim his right of "Fire and Salt" at a castle (the household accounts of Richard II show that every day ten thousand people sat down to meat at his charge, the royal kitchen serving out the messes to them by the hand of three hundred servitors) but even more he could expect hospitality at any religious house. This was the basic part of the religious life and was in some ways connected with the rights of sanctuary.

The Benedictine order, among others, had a specific rule that at each monastery an officer was appointed simply to look after guests. He was always to have on hand two tuns of wine for strangers and provender for their horses.

The monasteries had generally been endowed by the nobility who presented themselves seeking accommodation as a right for the establishment would be on their own lands or that of relatives or friends. This eventually led to abuse, as barons residing at home would send their followers down to the local abbey simply to save themselves the cost of feeding them.

Thus we have an account from Hampton showing an excessive expenditure on beer and bread "because the Duke of Cornwall lives near".

When hospitality was claimed to excess in this way it was usually because an heir considered that his father or other ancestor had made excessive donations to the religious order and so deprived him of his due inheritance. He could not upset such a bequest, but he could impose on the rules of hospitality to be an annoyance and embarrassment to the monastery.

Finally, Edward I forbade anyone to eat or lodge in a religious home unless he were formally invited and visiting magistrates were instructed to ask whether any lords or others "had sent into the houses or mansions belonging to the monks or others, men, horses or dogs to sojourn there at an expense not their own?" There was constant litigation in this connection.

The poorer traveller probably would not be received into the monastery proper as nobility was. Many establishments—as we see at Battle Abbey or Tewkesbury—had guest houses quite out-side the main buildings. Here the poor could eat or pass the night.

For those neither poor enough for charity nor rich enough to demand comfort in abbey or castle there were a few inns.

We have a record of three Fellows travelling from Oxford to Durham with four servants in 1331 and staying in inns over-night. A typical day's costs were:

Bread	4d.	Candles	$\frac{1}{4}$d.
Beer	2d.	Fuel	2d.
Wine	1$\frac{1}{4}$d.	Beds	2d.
Meat	5$\frac{1}{2}$d.	Fodder for	
Potage	$\frac{1}{4}$d.	horses	10d.

This might not seem excessive for seven people, but there were constant complaints of overcharging at inns. Edward III passed two statutes, the first useless and the second, four years later no better, to reduce "the great and outrageous cost of victuals kept up in all the realm by innkeepers and other retailers of victuals, to the great detriment of the people travelling across the realm".

Before this could happen there had to be some competition for custom and that meant there had to be more travellers.

In Jerusalem the Caliph Hakim destroyed the rebuilt Holy Sepulchre and started to harass the local Christians. The astute Greek Emperor Alexius Commenus had been, for some time, seeking allies to drive back the encroaching Turks and now he appealed to the Pope for help to drive out the Christian-harass-ing infidel. Pope Urban listened to the appeal with interest him-self. He knew that if such an expedition were launched, there could only be one leader, Pope Urban. This would establish his supremacy not only in Europe, but also perhaps the Eastern Church would return to the fold.

In 1095 Urban called on the Christians of Europe to avenge the desecration of the Holy Sepulchre, offering very attractive privileges—exemption from taxes, the rights of clergy in respect of legal processes and the like.

It was a call that made a universal appeal. The Normans had already carved up all the territory that was available in Europe. Younger sons, seeing little further chance of rapid advancement locally, were glad to be off. The ordinary freedman or yeoman perceived an unimagined opportunity to escape the life-long drudgery of the lower scales of feudalism.

As might have been expected bands of adventurers of this type were not easy to control.

"The servile peasantry, who for centuries had been bound to the glebe lands of Church and noble, whose sole occupation was the toil of labourer in the fields, swayed by the preaching of fanatical itinerant preachers of whom Peter the Hermit was the most notorious, ran away, en masse, leaving abandoned farms behind them. Whole villages were left deserted. Hordes of peasants, with their wives and children, together with a plentiful sprinkling of vagabond monks, runaway serfs, spendthrifts, speculators, prostitutes, boys and girls, fugitive criminals and the scum of medieval society, thronged the roads, pillaging farmsteads as they journeyed and sacking the Jewry in every town through which they passed. Fanaticism and avarice went hand in hand."

So started the Crusades which brought about the movement of masses across Europe and among other effects produced the Knights Hospitallers of St. John, the earliest order of knighthood and formed specifically to offer hospitality to travellers.

A hospice for pilgrims in Jerusalem had been dedicated in the eleventh century to St. John the Baptist. The head of this establishment was a certain Gerard who was able to assist the Crusaders from inside when they beseiged the Holy City in 1099.

After its capture he was naturally very popular and he took the opportunity to enlarge and improve the hospice. He then set up a new order—Knights of the Order of the Hospital of St. John of Jerusalem, under the immediate protection of the Pope and following the Augustinian rule.

Gerard died some twenty years later and Raymond du Puy succeeded as grand master of the order. He controlled it for about forty years and during this time established the order as a world power. They took over castles to be used as hospitals or hospices and were active in any battle to assist Christian pilgrims. Eventually they were driven out of the Holy Land and subsequently conquered Rhodes (then held by the Byzantines) and they watched the interests of pilgrims from there and supported any attack on Moslems.

They then moved to Malta—and are often known as the Knights of Malta—and continued to struggle with the Ottomans. France eventually took over Malta after the Revolution (when the Knights had unfortunately but not surprisingly sided with the French aristocracy) and the order in its old form virtually ceased. In England it had already suffered following the Reformation but offshoots live on in such worthy forms as the St. John's Ambulance Brigade.

This was one effect of the Crusades, another was the development of a greater interest in pilgrimages.

It might be noted that neither Pope Urban nor any of his contemporaries referred to the Holy Wars as "Crusades". They were regarded as armed pilgrimages.

There had been Christian pilgrimages to Bethlehem and Jerusalem as far back as the second century, but pilgrimages had been a feature of religious life from pre-history.

Pilgrimages had been made to Mecca for over a thousand years before Mohammed proclaimed that every Mussulman should visit Mecca at least once in his lifetime. In the fifth century B.C. the Koreshite tribe had organised the pilgrim traffic and built shelters for the caravan travellers. These included not only the Arabs, but also many Jews who believed that the temple which housed the Kaaba had been built by Abraham. Mohammed put a stop to the Jewish interest by having seven hundred of them slain, so preserving the shrine for the righteous.

It is a queer coincidence that both Islam and Christianity have their holy places in the same region. Not many of the faithful ever realize that whilst the Saracens were harassing the Christians, the activities of the Crusaders made it difficult for pious Mohammedans to visit their Mosque of Omar in Jerusalem.

Of course there had been a long period before this when both religions travelled peaceably together. As far back as the fourth century a great hospice had been created at Odessa in Greece to receive three hundred Christian pilgrims. This was later extended to accommodate up to a thousand.

Charlemagne established rest houses for pilgrims in the eighth century which even had what were described as latrines—a rarity in those days. Others also built hospices where the need arose in mountain passes. The original hospice of the Great St. Bernard's Pass, at a height of over 8,000 feet above sea level, was built in 961. St. Bernard, after whom the pass is named, was Charlemagne's uncle.

There were several orders of knighthood whose sole purpose was to protect the pilgrim and on popular pilgrim routes the religious orders seemed almost to have competed with each other in offering hospitality. On the road to Compostella, for instance, there was an abbey at Roncesvalles. The monks here advertised their services to pilgrims in a Latin poem. All who came were welcomed at the door, a man offered bread and took no price, within a barber and a cobbler were at the service of the pilgrims, the cellars were full of fruit and almonds, there were two hospices for the sick, with beds and baths, and if the pilgrim died there he would be buried in holy ground. Even today, what Hilton or Sheraton could compete with that?

Nevertheless the pilgrim's road was hard and dangerous and the journey long. So long, in fact, that in 1072 the Council of Rouen threatened to excommunicate all married women who prematurely announced the death of their husbands on pilgrimage in order to marry again. It is not established what would be "premature" but the pilgrimage to Jerusalem and back commonly took up seven years, so there was a good margin.

With all these dangers and difficulties it appeared to many prudent believers that a very satisfactory alternative to going on a pilgrimage was to despatch a paid substitute instead. This would be arranged during the lifetime of the devout one or even more frequently he would provide for it in his will. How could he put to better use the money he could not take with him?

The records show many old wills containing such bequests as:

May 2, 1388: John de Multon, Knight—My body to be Buried in the Monastery of the Blessed Mary of Lincoln . . . Item, I bequeath to one man going for my soul as far as Jerusalem, 5 marks, or

1417: Sir Richard Arundel, Knight, buried in St. Mary's Abbey, Rochester—My executors to find for the good of my soul to the Court of Rome, the Holy Land and the Sepulchre of Our Lord and to the Holy Blood in Germany, or

1400: Alice, Widow of Thomas Hose, Taverner—(I bequeath) to my son Thomas ten shillings to perform my pilgrimage to Walsingham.

A proportion, therefore, of any pilgrim band consisted of paid employees. These could easily be identified by the number of images and medals with which they were adorned. When a pilgrim reached his shrine he would purchase a little brooch or pewter medal as a memento. The professional did the same, so that as time passed he resembled a piece of luggage covered by hotel labels or the sticker-covered back windows of a British car.

Other pilgrims who might also appear to lack a certain devotion were those sent by authority. Often sinners had to make a pilgrimage as a penance for their misdeeds, but it was not just the Church that imposed these penalties. For example, at the conclusion of a dispute in 1356 the King of France stipulated in the peace treaty that three hundred men of Bruges and Cambrai had to make pilgrimages to Compostella and other places.

The average pilgrim band, therefore, was not likely to be distinguished by overmuch religious solemnity. William Thorpe, in fact, spoke most strongly on the matter when Archbishop Arundel examined him—a Lollard—in 1407.

He said that when "divers men and women" planned a pilgrimage they arranged beforehand:

"To have with them both men and women that can well sing wanton songs: and some other pilgrims who have with them bagpipes: so that every town that they come through, what with the noise of their singing and with the sound of their piping and with the jangling of their Canterbury bells and with the barking out of dogs after them, they make more noise than if the king came their way with all his clarions and many other minstrels. And if these men and women be a month out on their pilgrimage, many of them shall be a half year after great janglers, tale tellers and liars."

The Archbishop did not agree at all. "Lewd losel! thou seest not far enough in this matter. For thou considerest not the great travail of pilgrims, therefore, thou blamest the thing that is praiseworthy. I say to thee that it is right well done that pilgrims have with them both singers and also pipers; that when one of them that goeth barefoot striketh his toe against a stone and hurt him sore and maketh him to bleed, it is well done that he or his fellow begin then a song, or else take out of his bosom a bagpipe for to drive away with such mirth the hurt of his fellow for with such solace the travail and weariness of pilgrims is lightly and merrily borne out."

This might have been a very Christian view, but what the Church generally thought of pilgrimages may be gathered from the fact that nuns were forbidden to go on pilgrimages. It was forbidden as early as 791 and again in 1195 "In order that the opportunity of wandering may be taken from nuns we forbid them to take the path of pilgrimage," and again in 1318 nuns were told not to leave their convent "by reason of any vow of pilgrimage which they might have taken. If any had taken such vows she was to say as many psalters as it would have taken days to perform the pilgrimage rashly vowed." In other words, the Nonne, a Prioress y-cleped Madame Eglentyne who enjoyed a dance with their friar, should never have been on her way to Canterbury with Chaucer's merry band, at all.

The shrine at Canterbury was, of course, the tomb of St. Thomas à Becket and the other main shrine in England was our Lady of Walsingham. "The most holy name in all England" which attracted visitors from abroad to see "A crystal phial containing some milk of the virgin." They might have done better to have gone to Bethlehem where J. A. Jusserand tells us in his *English Wayfaring Life in the Middle Ages* in the Church of St. Nicholas "the sweet Virgin Mary hid herself to draw her milk from her worthy breasts when she would fly to Egypt. In this same church there is a marble column against which she leaned when she drew her worthy milk and the pillar continues moist since the time she leaned against it, and when it is wiped, at once it sweats again; and in all places where her worthy milk fell, the earth is still soft and white and has the appearance of curded milk, and whoever likes takes of it, out of devotion."

They might then have gone on to Constantinople to worship at the actual head of St. John the Baptist and perhaps compare it with the other actual head of St. John the Baptist in the church at Amiens.

Sometimes pilgrimages were not even ostensibly of religious intent. To visit the tomb of some rebel executed by the king was a satisfactory method of infuriating his majesty. Thus, when Simon de Montfort was killed he was actually under sentence of excommunication by the Church at the time, but still people flocked to his tomb and demanded that he should be canonized a saint.

Whatever the purpose of the pilgrimage it was very nearly the only reason for making a journey in the days when there was little inter-city or international trade. Thus most of the travel accommodation of that time was for pilgrims and it was not only the Church that provided this.

There were also guilds which kept open house to receive the pilgrims, always with the same object of joining themselves by some good work to that of the traveller. Thus the guild-merchants of Coventry, founded in 1340, maintained "a common lodging house of thirteen beds", to receive poor travellers who cross the country going on pilgrimage or from any other pious motive. This hostelry was directed by a governor, aided by a woman who washed the feet of the travellers and took care of them, Jusserand tells us.

Not everybody, however, had such a high regard for the pilgrim. Anybody with the scrip and staff was liable to attract the attention of the local sheriff. Far too many workmen would leave their masters to make a pilgrimage and happily take up new employment along the road when a better job offered. Eventually Richard II enacted that pilgrims who were fit and healthy had to carry a sort of passport and without this they were liable to arrest.

The Church itself had never been very happy about some of the pilgrims. Once they left home there tended to be a slackening of standards. Indeed the holy Bonifacius wrote to Cuthbert, Archbishop of Canterbury, a letter—which has since become famous—about the many women who made the pilgrimage to Rome and lost their virginity on the way, with the result that "in Gallia and in Lombardy there is literally not a single town left in which English women are not living as whores".

In time this urge to take the holy road would diminish, but through the fourteenth century the roads of Europe would have been empty but for the pilgrims. Inns would also have been empty had authority had its way: these establishments became no more popular with officialdom than they had ever been. In 1254 Louis IV had passed a law in France saying (Article 29) "No innkeeper shall lodge any individual except a transient or some-one having no establishment in the town."

In England Edward I was even more emphatic. In 1285 he passed a statute requiring taverns to shut at curfew because:

"Such offenders as aforesaid, going about by night do commonly resort and have their meetings and hold their evil talk in taverns more than elsewhere and there do seek the shelter, lying in wait and watching their time to do mischief."

It was about this time that the word "inn" came into its present use in England. Originally "inn" was a Saxon word meaning "chamber", but it came to mean a house. The inn as we know it today had to be described as a common inn just as today we speak of a *public* house. An ordinary inn (like an ordinary house today) was a private establishment. Sir Ronald Roxburgh quotes several documents referring to inns as houses or mansions. How many of the hundreds of thousands of Londoners who pass along Gray's Inn Road each day ever reflect that there once was a Gray's Inn? It was the house where Reginald de Grey (first Lord Grey of Wilton) lived in 1294—but it was an ordinary house, not a public house.

The Inns of Court are so named because in the thirteenth century lawyers took in their apprentices to live in their houses or inns (as employers generally did at that time) and as the students grew up they continued to congregate in communal dwellings convenient to the Palace at Westminster "as well for ease as decency, as also the better and more free access of the subject to advise. . . ."

Considering the interest of lawyers in the written word, early records are very sparse. For instance, we cannot ascertain whether Lincoln's Inn was the home of the Earl of Lincoln—as Stow assumed in his *Survey of London*, 1598—or Thomas de Lincoln, a sergeant-at-law—as E. Williams suggested in the *Atheneum* of 2nd September, 1906.

There is an odd feature in the translation of the Bible in 1534. Luke ii. 7 said simply "She layed him in a manger because there was no rume for them within in the ynne."

It is very interesting that the Modern Version reads ". . . in the manger because there was no room for them to lodge in the house". House is an accurate transcription of the 1534 word *ynne* but neither reflect the word in the original text—*Katalumati*. This is used three times in the Bible, always with the meaning of a common inn. Indeed there is an associated verb meaning to ruin oneself (by debauchery).

Did the sixteenth-century churchmen shy away from associating the Holy Family with a common inn and their twentieth-century successors too? It seems possible for *inn* was still being used to refer to a private house and not *Katalumati* long after 1534—Shakespeare published the *Tragedy of King Richard the Second* in 1598 and he has Richard's mother actually using the word *inn* as a mansion in contrast to an ale-house (Act V, Sc. 1).

> . . . thou most beauteous inn,
> Why should hard-favoured grief be lodged in thee,
> When triumph is become an ale-house guest?

It does not seem likely that we will ever imitate the later Elizabethans and drop the word *public*, referring to our taverns just as *houses.* The abbreviation *pub* is now established as our shortened term.

Whilst the roads in Europe were so empty the situation in the East was quite different. By a freak of chance we have a vivid picture of life there. Shortly after he returned from his travels in Tartary Marco Polo was captured by the Genoese and thrown into prison. By great good fortune a fellow prisoner was a writer, Rustician, and the two whiled away their time by getting on to paper an account of life in far Cathay under the Great Khan.

He lived in a splendour that even Tiberius might have envied. "On account of the narrowness of the passes in some parts of the country where the grand khan follows the chase, he is borne upon two elephants only, or sometimes a single one, being more convenient than a greater number; but under other circumstances he makes use of four, upon the backs of which is placed a pavilion of wood, handsomely carved, the inside being lined with cloth of gold, and the outside covered with the skins of lions, a mode of conveyance which is rendered necessary to him during his hunting excursions, in consequence of the gout, with which he is troubled. In the pavilion he always carried with him twelve of his best gerfalcons, with twelve officers, from amongst his favourites, to bear him company and amuse him. Those who are on horseback by his side give him notice of the approach of cranes or other birds, upon which he raises the curtain of the pavilion, and when he espies the game, gives direction for letting fly the gerfalcons, which seize the cranes and overpower them after a long struggle. The view of this sport, as he lies upon his couch, affords extreme satisfaction to his majesty, as well as to the officers who attend him, and to the horsemen by whom he is surrounded. After having thus enjoyed the amusement for some hours, he repairs to a place named Kakzarnodin, where are pitched the pavilions and tents of his sons, and also of the nobles, the lifeguards, and the falconers; exceeding ten thousand in number, and making a handsome appearance. The tent of his majesty, in which he gives his audiences, is so long and wide that under it ten thousand soldiers might be drawn up, leaving room for the superior officers and other persons of rank. Its entrance fronts the south, and on the eastern side it has another tent connected with it, forming a capacious saloon, which the emperor usually occupies, with a few of his nobility, and when he thinks proper to speak to any other persons, they are introduced to him in that apartment. In the rear of this there is a large and handsome chamber, where he sleeps; and there are many other tents and apartments (for the different branches of the household), but which are not immediately connected with the great tent. These halls and chambers are all constructed and fitted up in the following manner. Each of them is supported by three pillars of wood, richly carved and gilt. The tents are covered on the outside with the skins of lions, streaked white, black and red, and so well joined together that neither wind nor rain can penetrate. Withinside they are lined with the skins of ermines and sables, which are the most costly of all furs; for the latter, if of a size to trim a dress, is valued at two thousand besants of gold, provided it be perfect, but if otherwise, only one thousand. It is esteemed by Tartars the queen of furs. The animal, which in their language is named rondes, is about the size of a polecat. With these two kinds of skin, the halls as well as the sleeping-rooms are handsomely fitted up in compartments, arranged with much taste and skill. The tent-ropes, or cords by which they stretch the tents, are all of silk. Near to the grand tent of his majesty are situated those of his ladies, also very handsome and splendid. They have in like manner their gerfalcons, their hawks, and other birds and beasts, with which they partake in the amusement. The number of persons collected in these encampments is quite incredible, and a spectator might conceive himself to be in the midst of a populous city, so great is the assemblage from every part of the empire. The grand Khan is attended on the occasion by the whole of his family and household; that is to say, his physicians, astronomers, falconers, and every other description of officer."

Here again we have the picture of the great "camping out" because no ordinary hostelry could offer such luxury.

Old Cathay did have good hostels though and we have a description of the Great Khan's posting system which appears to have been even better than that of Imperial Rome, with post-houses every twenty-five or thirty miles.

"These are large and handsome buildings, having several well-furnished apartments, hung with silk, and provided with everything suitable to persons of rank. Even kings may be lodged at these stations in a becoming manner, as every article required may be obtained from the towns and strong places in the vicinity; and for some of them the court makes regular provision. At each station four hundred good horses are kept in constant readiness . . . no fewer than two hundred thousand horses are thus employed in the department of the post, and ten thousand buildings, with suitable furniture, are kept up. It is indeed so wonderful a system, and so effective in its operation, as it is scarcely possible to describe. If it be questioned how the population of the country can supply sufficient numbers for these duties, and by what means they can be victualled, we may answer, that all the idolators, and likewise the Saracens, keep six, eight, or ten women, according to their circumstances, by whom they have a prodigious number of children; some of them as many as thirty sons capable of following their fathers in arms; whereas with us a man has only one wife, and even although she should prove barren, he is obliged to pass his life with her, and is by that means deprived of the chance of raising a family. Hence it is that our population is so much inferior to theirs. . . ."

Every three miles there were little villages where lived foot messengers who ran to the next village with bells on their clothing to warn the next courier to be ready. So "in the course of two days and two nights his majesty receives distant intelligence that in the ordinary mode could not be obtained in less than ten days and it often happens that in the fruit season, what is gathered in the morning at Kanbalu is conveyed to the Grand Khan, at Shan-du, by the evening of the following day; although the distance is generally considered ten days' journey. At each of these three-mile stations there is a clerk, whose business it is to note the day and hour at which the one courier arrives and the other departs; which is likewise done at all the post-houses. Besides this, officers are directed to pay monthly visits to every station, in order to examine into the management of them. . . . When it is necessary that the messengers should proceed with extraordinary despatch, as in the cases of giving information of disturbance in any part of the country, the rebellion of a chief, or other important matter, they ride two hundred, or sometimes two hundred and fifty miles in the course of a day. On such occasions they carry with them the tablet of the gerfalcon as a signal of the urgency of their business and the necessity for despatch. And when there are two messengers, they take their departure together from the same place, mounted upon good fleet horses; and they gird their bodies tight, bind a cloth round their heads, and push their horses to the greatest speed. They continue thus till they come to the next post-house, at twenty-five miles distant, where they find two other horses, fresh and in a state for work; they spring upon them without taking any repast, and changing in the same manner at every stage, until the day closes, they perform a journey of two hundred and fifty miles. In cases of great emergency they continue their course during the night, and if there should be no moon, they are accompanied to the next station by persons on foot, who run before them with lights; when, of course, they do not make the same expedition as in the day-time, the light-bearers not being able to exceed a certain pace. Messengers qualified to undergo this extraordinary degree of fatigue are held in high estimation."

It seems quite clear that this official system was for the use only of government officials, ambassadors and the like and no doubt the Polo family, who were held in high esteem by Ghengis Khan, would have this privilege.

Even without it, however, the traveller had better facilities in Asia than in any other part of the world at that time, for trade was brisk. Indeed as we have already seen (page 14) some of the amenities offered to travellers startled the worthy Venetians.

"The inhabitants of this district are in the shameful and odious habit of considering it no mark of disgrace that those who travel through the country should have connection with their wives, daughters or sisters; but, on the contrary, when strangers arrive, each householder endeavours to conduct one of them home, and, giving up all the females of the family to him, leaves him in the situation of master of the house, and takes his departure. And while the stranger is in the house, he places a signal at the window as his hat or some other thing; and as long as this signal is seen in the house, the husband remains absent. And this custom prevails throughout that province. This they do in honour of their idols, believing that by such acts of kindness and hospitality to travellers a blessing is obtained, and that they shall be rewarded with a plentiful supply of the fruits of the earth."

One suspects that the old Italian was writing for his public. He had spent a long time in Asia and knew well that the standards of Venice were far from accepted in Tartary. For instance, having a high opinion of his own worth, he was shocked by one practice he came across:

"Before the time of their becoming subject to the dominion of the grand Khan, these people (in Karazan) were addicted to the following brutal custom. When any stranger of superior quality, who united personal beauty with distinguished valour, happened to take up his abode at the house of one of them, he was murdered during the night; not for the sake of his money, but in order that the spirit of the deceased, endowed with his accomplishments and intelligence might remain with the family, and that through the efficacy of such an acquisition all their concerns might prosper. Accordingly, the individual was accounted fortunate who possessed in this manner the soul of any noble personage: and many lost their lives in consequence. But from the time of His Majesty's beginning to rule the country, he has taken measure for suppressing the horrid practice, and from the effect of severe punishments that have been inflicted, it has ceased to exist."

Whenever we can check on what the great traveller wrote we find generally that he is accurate, so presumably there is some truth even in this grisly story. Generally, however, Marco found compensations for the traveller in Tartary. From Tebeth, for example, he smacks his lips over

". . . a scandalous custome which could only proceed from the blindness of idolatry, prevails among the people of these parts, who are disinclined to marry young women so long as they are in their virgin state, but require, on the contrary, that they should have had previous commerce with many of the other sex; and this, they assert, is pleasing to their deities, and that a woman who has not had the company of men is worthless. Accordingly, upon the arrival of a caravan of merchants, and as soon as they have set up their tents for the night, those others who have marriageable daughters conduct them to the place, and each, contending for a preference, entreats the strangers to accept of her daughter and enjoy her society so long as they remain in the neighbourhood. Such as have most beauty to recommend them are, of course, chosen, and the others return home disappointed and chagrined, whilst the former continue with the travellers until the period of their departure. They then restore them to their mothers, and never attempt to carry them away. It is expected, however, that the merchants should make them presents of trinkets, rings or other complimentary tokens of regard, which the young women take home with them. When, afterwards, they are designed for marriage, they wear all these ornaments about the neck or other part of the body, and she who exhibits the greatest number of them is considered to have attracted the attention of the greatest number of men, and is on that account in the higher estimation with the young men who are looking out for wives; then can she bring to her husband a more acceptable portion than a quantity of such gifts. At the solemnization of her nuptials she accordingly makes a display of them to the assembly, and he regards them as a proof that their idols have rendered her lovely in the eyes of men. From henceforward no person can dare to meddle with her who has become the wife of another and this rule is never infringed."

As Marco might well have said, one half of the world did not know how the other half lived.

A century and a half after he had sat in his prison in Genoa, accurately recalling detail after detail from his fantastic memory, another man sat in the same city intently reading the great book. As he read he scribbled notes and over seventy pages of the book are marked—you can see it today in the Columbina at Seville.

The reader was a sea captain and he knew that whilst the Polos had been able to travel freely into Asia by simply heading East this was no longer possible. The peoples of Islam were antagonistic again and the ruling Chinese dynasty itself was now anti-foreign. There was no possibility of going East but if, as was claimed, the world was round; then he could still reach the same gold roofed palaces of Cipangu by sailing West. That, Columbus decided, was his obvious course.

SHEPHEARD'S HOTEL *The top picture shows this great hotel as the majority of people know it, with the famous terrace. It was actually the third building occupied by Shepheard's—the last point of civilisation to be seen by the traveller to the east, and the first to welcome him back. Unfortunately this building was burnt down in the rioting in 1952. The lower picture shows its replacement, the fourth in a distinguished line of Shepheard's Hotels. It was said that the fame of the original Shepheard's outdid that of the pyramids. Eventually, perhaps, the size will also.*

(*Above*) THE IMPERIAL HOTEL *This is opposite the Imperial Palace in Tokyo. Designed by Frank Lloyd Wright with a special construction to avoid earthquakes, it was quickly put to the test. In 1923 a particularly bad tremor razed most of Tokyo but the hotel stood intact. It is now preserved by government order despite constant efforts by commercial interests to replace it. Failing this (below), this great annexe has been built at the rear.*

CHAPTER 4

MERRIE ENGLAND

The ancient, true and proper use of Inns, Ale Houses and Victual-
ling Houses is for the Receipt, Relief and Lodging of Wayfaring
People, travelling from place to place and not meant for the entertainment and harbouring of Lewd and Idle People to spend and
consume their Money and Time in Lewd and Drunken Manner.

Act of 1604

IN Europe lack of custom was holding up development of the inn
before the fifteenth century. Whilst the pilgrims and vagrants
enjoyed free charity and the nobility expected free hospitality
there could not be much general demand for good inns, for the
few middle-class travellers.

In Scotland (then a separate kingdom from England, of course)
the situation was even worse. The Scots had maintained the old
tradition of private hospitality long after it had withered in
England. Perhaps to assist the innkeeper, but more likely to keep
a check on the movement of travellers, a statute, probably unique
in the world, was passed in 1425. Travellers were liable to a
penalty of forty shillings (a very big sum then) if they took abode
with friends when there was an inn available. The only exception
was made for a nobleman accompanied by his retinue; he could
stay where he pleased, but his servants and horses had to be
quartered in the "common hostelries".

These in both England and Scotland must usually have been
very rough. "The times could still be remembered," wrote
William Harrison in his *Description of Britain* (1577), "when the
goodman of the house made his fire against the reredoes of his
hall", and lay upon straw with a log for a bolster, covered only

3—TPOTP

in "Dog-swain and hopharlots". As for servants, there was not much nightwear over or under "to keep them from the prickling of the straws that ran often through the canvas and razed their hardened hides". The inns themselves Thomas Burke tells us in *The English Inn* "had stone or earthen floors strewn with rushes. In the main room a number of mattresses were laid around the walls, and here the guests slept. Meals were individual matters. Instead of sitting at the great table and sharing a common meal, as at the church-houses, each man ate such food as he had with him or could purchase from the house. Bread, meat and beer was the usual fare; varied occasionally by fish or capon".

Privacy was no more expected in an inn than it is now in an omnibus. It was taken for granted that an establishment of ten or twelve rooms could accommodate two hundred visitors, sleeping on the floor or where they could. When beds were provided they were communal affairs with guests sleeping "spoon fashion". In *Twelfth Night* Shakespeare mentions the great Bed of Ware which slept sixty-eight people. James Fosbrook later presented it to King Edward.

There was no suggestion of any segregation of the sexes in this communal sleeping. In his *English Inn Signs* J. Larwood tells us of the Scole Inn where "There was lately a very round bed, big enough to hold fifteen or twenty couples in imitation (I suppose) of the remarkable Great Bed at Ware".

Another aspect of English inn-keeping we might find surprising today, aroused the comment of foreign visitors—the warmth of the welcome of the English female. In 1466 Leo Van Rozmital paid us a visit and noted in his diary "when guests arrive at an inn the hostess and all her family go out to meet and receive them and guests are required to kiss them all". Thirty years later Erasmus was writing to the same effect "You are received with a kiss by all; when you take your leave, you are dismissed with kisses; you return, kisses are repeated. They come to visit you, kisses again; they leave you, you kiss them all round . . . in fine, wherever you move, there is nothing but kisses."

When contemplating the warmth of these greetings in the good old days, it is as well to recall that this was a time when any woman who had escaped smallpox was a beauty and bad teeth were as common as fleas.

Whilst the welcome at religious hostels might not be so warm, there is evidence that the standard of accommodation could be vastly better than one would expect.

We are fortunate in having a very full account of the running of the Savoy Hospital. This was established by Henry VII in 1509 on the Savoy site, where John O'Gaunt's castle once stood. (The Hospital chapel still stands today and many visitors think it is the chapel of the earlier palace.) Basically there was one huge dormitory, together with kitchens, offices, etc. Provision was made for the appointment of the master and also a matron, receiving a yearly allowance of £4 6s. 8d. for her living expenses and clothing. She had twelve women under her who were required to be thirty-six years of age and over, unmarried and "with as many virgins among them as possible".

All the staff wore a special uniform and the intention of the hospital was to provide overnight accommodation for one night's lodging. However, nothing in the Statutes prevented a man coming back night after night, and as might have been expected, this eventually caused a great deal of trouble.

Every evening at an hour before sunset the matron, one of her assistants, and a porter stood at the great gate of the hospital facing into the Strand to receive the poor. They were required to give preference to sick persons other than lepers.

When a man entered he went straight to the chapel for a prayer and was then passed to the hot baths and provided with temporary clothing whilst his own clothing was put in a special oven for de-lousing.

The men could then engage in "modest conversations" by the fireside—there were two in the winter—and at eight o'clock in the winter or at ten o'clock in the summer they had to turn in.

In the dormitory were a hundred beds with flock mattresses and feather beds, bolsters and pillows. Three pairs of sheets and two pairs of blankets were provided for each bed, together with a linen coverlet and a counterpane. Around each bed was a curtain matching the counterpane. This curtain could be pulled right round to screen the bed. At either end and in the middle of the dormitory lamps were left burning all night.

Fifteen times at five o'clock in the morning the great bell of the chapel tolled and again at six o'clock when mass was celebrated. All the inmates had to be up and out by seven in the summer or eight in the winter. Any who were sick remained in bed and were visited by the doctor and a surgeon and also the chaplain or one of his assistants called twice a day.

The standard set appears far better than one would have expected. Unfortunately, what was intended by Henry VII and what occurred in practice were perhaps not always identical and so we find in 1535 a commission set up to enquire the state of the hospital and whether there was any discrimination in taking in "suche as they reken most clene of the poore and repell them that they reken most sore or diseased, for avoydyng of their own loathesomeness or contageon". There were questions on hygiene; did any poor man lie in unwashed sheets that had been used by another? Did they sleep more than one a bed? We do not know what were the answers to these questions—the interesting point is that they should ever have been asked at all. Clean sheets for the sick and the poor? The British Army was not to consider providing sheets (or pyjamas) for its ordinary soldiers for more than another four centuries.

The standards set for the Savoy Hospital seem to have been extraordinarily high for those times, when the average peasant was still sleeping in straw.

The better type of inn would allow more freedom and perhaps better company, but the actual furnishings were austere.

There is a record in the archives at Salisbury of a lease dated 9th April, 1473, to John Gryme, a saddler, and it is of interest because it describes the rooms in the *George Inn* (it is still in business) and gives an inventory of the furniture. There were thirteen guest chambers. The practice of simply numbering hotel rooms is a comparatively modern one and at the *George* the rooms were—the Principal Chambers, the Earl's Chamber, the Pantry adjoining, the Oxford, the Abingdon, the Squire's, the

Lombard, the Garret, the George, the Clarendon, the Understent, the Fitzwaryn and the London Chamber.

There was also the Buttery, Kitchen, Tap House, the Parlour, Hostry and Wine Cellar.

Each room is supplied with three beds, trestle tables for eating and wooden forms. The Principal Chamber also had a cupboard, but none of the others did, and that was the inventory. Homeliness rather than luxury was the theme.

The Church not only tempted travellers away from the accommodation offered at the inn, but also took a lively interest in the drink trade. In the Middle Ages in England the monks brewed ale with the same care and skill that today they give to distilling the great liqueurs from their secret recipes.

> The Abbot of Burton brewed good ale
> On Fridays when they fasted,
> But the Abbot of Burton never tasted his own,
> As long as his neighbours' lasted.

We do not know who was the careful Abbot, but it is thanks to him and his kin that Burton is famous today—even if not for piety.

A point about this brewing in religious houses is made by F. W. Hackwood in *Inns, Ales and Drinking Customs*.

"To the association of ale-brewing with monastic life we owe the familiar marking of beer barrels with X or XX or XXX. These marks came to be interpreted as signifying the relative alcoholic strength of the drink and people came to speak of 'double X' and 'treble X' as we now speak of Pale, Mild or Strong ales. But the custom of marking barrels in this way arose in former times when monasteries were recognized brewing centres, the original idea being that of a sort of trade mark guarantee; for in shape the crosses were, at first, more akin to the crucifix and served to indicate by the oath of the monks, 'Sworn on the cross', the beer was of sound quality, fit to drink."

This seems a very far fetched explanation—why should the monks take an oath and if they did why should they mark the X on the cask? Is there any evidence that early X's were crucifix shaped? More likely is the suggestion that the X's date from the imposition of excise duty. The tax on strong beer then was 2s. 6d. a barrel and this might well have been marked XXX.

Whilst the origin of the X is doubtful there is every evidence that the brewer and cellarer in the old religious houses were important officials and in the Priory at Winchester special prayers were offered up for them.

Perhaps they should have done this at Dunstable too for the records show that "about the feast of St. John the Baptist, our ale failed". Twelve years later the same thing happened, but they were learning, "At the Feast of Pentecost our malt failed. We drank five casks of wine and it did us much good."

Brewing outside the Church was often in female hands. In the home it certainly was, right into the seventeenth century.*

Ladies who were in the business professionally were called brewsters—the feminine of brewer. Why the word lingers on in "Brewster Sessions" (the licensing courts) is not clear except perhaps for euphony.

Ale-wives were far from popular and Elynour Rummynge of Leatherhead appears to have been regarded as typical. Skelton, tutor to King Henry VIII, immortalized her—

> Her face all bowsy
> Comely crynkled
> Wondrously wrinkled,
> Like a rost pigges ears,
> Brystled with hair,
> Her nose somdele hoked
> And camously croked
> Never stoppynge
> But ever dropping . . .
> She breweth noppy ale
> And maketh thereof fast sale
> To travellers, to tinkers
> And all good ale drinkers.

* Alreach, King of Hordoland, is said to have chosen Geirhild for his queen "in consequence of her proficiency in this necessary art", Mr. Bicker-dyke tells us. One has a pleasing picture of the good king pottering back to the palace with beery breath and the chamberlain whispering to some noble, "Courting again".

Generally either men or women might brew ale just as either might bake bread today. However, ale brewing seems to have been a good deal more contentious than bread making. There were innumerable disputes about the quality of the brews. The position got so bad in Oxford in 1434 that all the brewers were assembled and each made to swear on the Blessed Evangelists to brew good ale and wholesome "So far as his ability and human frailty permits".

They certainly seem to have been frail. In 1449 we find that nine brewers have brewed "an ale of little or no strength, to the grave and no mean damage of the University and town, and that they are obstinate and rebels and refuse to serve the principals and others of the Halls with ale". We do not know what happened to them but later we find John Janyn ordered to refund to Anisia Barbour the sum of 8d. because he had sold her a cask of ale for 20d. and "in our opinion and that of others who have just tasted it, it is not worth more than 12d.".

We may smile at the serious tone of these old charges but at this time ale was part of the staple diet of the English and not merely a thirst quencher or basis for a night out.

". . . such good strong beer as shall be most cherishing to poor labouring people, without which they cannot well subsist: their food being for the most part of such things as afford little or bad nourishment, nay, sometimes dangerous; and would infect them with many sicknesses and diseases, were they not preserved (as with an antidote), with good beer, whose virtues and effectual operations, by the help of the hop well boiled in it, are more powerful to expel poisonous infections than is yet publicly known."

As this was part of a petition drafted by the brewers we need not regard it as strictly accurate, but it does indicate the outlook at that time. Not only did ale form part of the diet then but, before the introduction of tea or coffee, an astonishingly large part.

When one thinks of a Maid of Honour at Court one tends to picture a dainty, perhaps coy, little lady. One is not likely to think of her putting away as a regular thing two gallons of ale for her breakfast. And yet it is clearly laid down in the Ordinances of Eltham, 17, Henry VIII, that Maids of Honour of the Queen are each allowed for breakfast, "one chet lofe, one manchet (a bread roll) two gallons of ale, dim pitcher of wine".

It might be thought that a lot of this drink would be handed down to other servants but when Pulteney, later Earl of Bath, was dying the greatest physicians in the land were summoned. All pronounced his case hopeless.

"Whilst those gathered round the bedside of the supposed dying man listened for his last sigh, he faintly murmured, 'Small beer, small beer'. The doctors did not think it worth while to say nay, and a half gallon cup of small beer was put to the lips of the sick man, who drained it to the dregs, and then demanded another draught, which was served in the same way: then turning on his side, he went off into a deep slumber, attended with profuse perspiration, and awoke a new man."

This is quoted (*Chambers Journal* 2/1/1875) in connection with the beneficial effects of ale drinking but our interest is the quantity consumed. When this dying man wants a drink there is no fooling around with a medicine glass—he is offered a half-gallon. These were the days when people were able to think big.

Again in the records of the Earl of Northumberland in 1512 it is shown that each child in the nursery had for breakfast, "a manchet, a quart of beer, a dish of butter, a piece of salt fish and a dish of sprats". In the evening the Earl and his lady sat down to "two manchetts, a loaf of bread, a gallon of beer and a quart of wine".

One might reasonably assume that the gallon at that time measured less than our gallon today. Surprisingly the reverse is the case. Apart from the grain measure there were two gallons in Tudor times: the Wine Gallon and the Ale Gallon. The Wine Gallon was eighty per cent of our present Imperial Gallon but the Ale Gallon was 282 cubic inches against the 277.4 cubic inches of the present Imperial Gallon. Elizabeth's original Bronze Exchequer Standard Measures are all to be seen in the Science Museum in London.

When we read Queen Elizabeth's accounts and see that as well as vast quantities of ale and beer she also had regularly every morning a pint of wine for her breakfast, we begin to wonder whether the phrase "Merrie Englande" has perhaps a rather different connotation from the one we had always assumed.

It is interesting to see in the brewers' petition the reference to the hop. The early part of the sixteenth century was absorbed in religious dispute, Papal bulls, schisms and dogma and very unpleasant it must have been.

At the same time there was another bitter dispute about beer and ale. The normal method of brewing ale for centuries had simply required hot water pouring over the malt mash, boiling up the resulting liquid for an hour or so, the froth was skimmed off, yeast added and then in a very short time the ale sold— early in Elizabeth's reign it was laid down that the brewers should not deliver their liquors until eight hours after it had been tunned in the summer and six hours in the winter.

The brewers were anxious to move it quickly for this easily made liquid was always liable to go sour. In any case it appears to have been a plain uninspiring sort of a drink and the tendency was for all who could afford it to spice their ale much as they spiced their cakes. However, not many had the means for this and as long as any spilt ale was thick enough to stick the cup to the table, it was acceptable.

The risk of the ale going sour was much reduced by boiling hops up with it and this drink was called beer. This use of hops had been known for centuries—Pliny mentions it in his *Natural History*—and in their Babylonian captivity the Jews had regarded it as a protection against leprosy. Hops had been used in England but not very much before 1520. Then

> Hops Reformation bays and beer
> Came into England all in one year.

English soldiers fighting in the Low Countries developed a taste for spirits and something stronger than the unsophisticated English ale. The Dutch used hops and the returned soldiers still wanted them and eventually Flemings settled in Kent to grow the bitter tasting plant and its use spread slowly.

The more conservative drinker regarded beer with the same horror as his counterpart today has for beer in cans.

In Richard III's reign the Brewers' Company petitioned Lord Mayor Billesden against ". . . puttying of hoppes and other things in the said ale, contrary to the good and holesome manner of bruynge of ale of old tyme used . . . to the great deceite and hurt of the King's liege people . . . pleas it therefore your saide good lordshyppe to forbit the putting into ale of any hops, herbs or any other like thing, but onely licour malte and yeste."

Andrew Boorde in his *Dyetary* made the whole position quite clear in 1542.

"Ale for an Englyssheman is a naturall drinke . . . Barley malt maketh better ale than oten malte or any other corne doth: it doth ingendre grose humoures: but yette it maketh a man stronge.

"Beer is made of malte, of hoppes and water; it is the naturell drynke for a Dutche man and now of late dayes it is moche used in Englande to the detryment of many Engleysshe people; specyally it killeth them that be troubled with the colycke and the stone for the drink is a colde drynke: yet it doth make a man fat, and doth inflate the bely, as it doth appere by the Dutche men's faces and Belyes."

Henry VIII, as fat as any Dutch beer drinker one would have thought, forbade his brewer to use hops and it was more than a hundred years before beer became accepted as the Englysshe-man's naturell drynke.

Meantime the inn was still struggling for the traveller's custom. Presumably the small merchant or the lower professional classes who could not depend on hospitality in the mansions and were not eligible for religious charity on their business travels would look to the inns for their accommodation. Even in this trade, however, there could be difficulty for various guilds or trade associations often interfered with the freedom of their members to stay where they wanted.

The Merchants of the Staple, for example, controlled the wool trade—Britain's greatest business at that time. The wool merchants were generally based on the Cotswolds and every year would travel to the Continent with their bales to sell them. Any merchant of consequence would know Calais very well, but English merchants there could not live where they liked. The Company of the Staple had a list of regular licensed lodgings where the merchants had to stay, rather as a university licenses lodgings for its students. (Do not forget that at this time Calais was not French, but part of the English kingdom.)

There is reference to some old dispute about these lodgings in the Cely Papers.

"Item. Sir, please it you to understand that here is a variance betwixt our host, Thomas Graunger and the fellowship, of our lodging, for Thomas Graunger promised us at his coming in to our lodging that we should pay no more for our board but 3s. 4d. a week at the high table and 2s. 6d. at the side table, and now he saith he will have no less than 4s. a week at the high table and 40 pence at the side table, wherefore the fellowship here will depart into other lodgings, some to one place and some to another."

Far more surprising were the arrangements of the Hanseatic League for its members. This federation of German merchants had acquired many privileges over the years from various European monarchs. They had customs and tax concessions and operated as a tight little commercial empire that dominated trade and commerce throughout Europe for generations.

In London they lived in what was called "The Steelyard". Cornelius Walford tells us it was "of considerable extent and at one period protected by high and strong walls and probably fortified ... These early Steelyard merchants ... conducted their affairs with the utmost secrecy and lived personally in a state of entire seclusion, like the inmates of a monastery. Indeed, the Steelyard was a monastery—the only difference being that its brotherhood were devoted to money-making instead of religious exercises. The vast buildings on the river side in the parts not used for storage were divided into separate cells for single men— the whole of the ranges opening into common reception rooms. No inmate of the Steelyard was allowed to marry, or even to visit any person of the opposite sex, and a breach of this law, however slight, was followed by immediate expulsion, if not by more severe penalties. At a fixed hour every evening all the brothers were expected to be at home, the gates were then rigidly closed; and at a certain hour in the morning, varying with the seasons, were open again for the transaction of business."

These arrangements must have been abnormal, but it is quite clear that many of the merchant class, on whose patronage the inns might depend, went elsewhere.

From this time then, date not our oldest inns but the hostels that were to become the oldest inns still standing. The *George and Pilgrim Inn* at Glastonbury, for example, was built by Abbot John de Selwood to accommodate pilgrims and other visitors to the Abbey. The *New Inn* at Gloucester, the *George* at Winchcombe, the *Star* at Alfriston, the *Angel* at Walsingham and the *Red Lion* at Colchester all date from this period.

Similarly the gentry were starting to erect outhouses on their estates to accommodate the retinues of their guests and these would also develop into regular inns.

Presumably this trend would have developed steadily as it did on the continent and the inns would have grown slowly, side by side with the religious hostels.

It was not to be so in England. When Pope Urban declared that the infidel should be ousted from the Holy City he started the Crusades that resulted in chains of religious hostels across Europe. When Pope Clement declared that Henry's first wife, Catherine, could not be ousted from their state of holy wedlock he started the movement that closed the religious hospices throughout England.

When the Dissolution was complete six hundred and fifty-five monasteries, ninety colleges and one hundred and ten hospitals, about a twentieth of the whole national estate, had been suppressed and the income dissipated. This tore great gaps in the travellers' social services.

With the charitable monks no longer offering a roof and a crust there was an immediate and pressing need for more inns. At first travellers were often reduced to making use of derelict church buildings and the like, but conditions soon improved as the need showed the opportunity. Often the steward of an old suppressed hospice would set up an inn on a busy thoroughfare, sometimes in the same building.

The hostels that had been attached to the abbeys such as the George Inn at Winchcombe or the Manor of God-Begot at Winchester became secular inns.

Old inn signs are often a guide to an origin linked to the Church. The *Priory Arms* at Folkestone, for instance, once stood opposite a former priory. The *Goat and Compasses* is said to be derived from "God encompasseth us", although Larwood thinks this far-fetched. Undoubtedly, however, *The Bull* as a sign has nothing to do with the Roast Beef of Old Englande but is a corruption from La Boule (or Latin Bulla) the seal of a monastery.

The *Crossed Keys* are often the insignia of an abbot and the *King's Head* might well have been the *Pope's Head* before the Reformation.

No great churches were built by the Tudors but many of our most famous old inns date from this period.

The custom for the larger houses was to build around three sides of the inn yard and each floor would have a balcony over the yard. Visitors had rooms giving on to the balconies so all could look out and enjoy the movement and bustle of a coach coming or going. They were simple times but should this excitement pall the amphitheatre-like arrangement of the inn yard made it a perfect setting for such entertainments as bear baiting or, in Spain, bullfighting.

Until James Burbage built one in 1576, there was no such thing as a theatre in Britain. Strolling players set up their stages —boards resting on barrels or trestles—wherever they could and these galleried inn yards were favourite sites.

As a result when theatres did come to be built they were not more than enlarged inn yards—the pit, balconies and boxes merely being developments of the original yard and galleries.

The *George* at Southwark is the only example of this type of building left in London now, but there are a few others around the country—the *New Inn* at Gloucester is an excellent example.

We get a good picture of the *White Hart,* Southwark's oldest inn, by Charles Dickens in Pickwick. He was writing of a later period, of course, but the picture had not changed.

". . . a double tier of bedroom galleries, with old clumsy ballustrades run around two sides of the straggling area, and a double row of bells to correspond, sheltered from the weather by a little sloping roof, hung over the door leading to the bar and coffee room. Two or three gigs and chaise carts were wheeled up under different little sheds and pent houses: and the occasional heavy tread of a cart-horse or rattling of a chain at the far end of the yard announced to anybody who cared about the matter that the stable lay in that direction. When we add that a few boys in smock frocks were lying asleep on heavy packages, wool packs, and other articles that were scattered about on heaps of straw, we have described as fully as need be the general appearance of . . ."

Writing in 1598, Stowe gives us a fine account of the inns at Southwark, a borough which a later State paper states "consists chiefly of inn-keepers". This concentration, probably the heaviest in the world at that time, was due to Southwark's situation on the high road to Dover and Canterbury. Wagons and stage wagons could unload there near the City without the delay and trouble of crossing London Bridge.

"From thence towards London Bridge," writes Stow, "bee many faire Innes, for receit of travellers by these signes the *Spurre, Christopher, Bull, Queens Head, Tabard, George, Hart, King's Head,* etc. Amongst which the most ancient is the *Tabard,* so called of the signe, which as wee now terms it, is of a Jacket or sleeveless coate whole before, open on both sides, with a square collar, winges at the shoulders: a stately garment, of olde time commonly worne of noblemen and others, both at home and abroad in the warres: but then (to wit in the warres) their Arme embroidered, or otherwise depict upon them that every man by his coate of armes might be knowne from others: But now these Tabards are only worn by the Heralds, and bee called their coates of Armes in service. . . ."

These inn signs were the subject of constant legislation. There is a record of a Chelsea ale wife being prosecuted in 1393 for failing to exhibit an ale-stake although she sold ale. In the reign of Henry V the position had so changed that the Common Council ordained that "whereas the ale-stakes projecting in front of taverns in Chepe, and elsewhere in the said City, extended too far over the King's Highways, to the impeding of riders and others, and by reason of their excessive weight, to the great deterioration of the houses to which they are fixed," these stakes should not extend more than seven feet over the King's Highway.

However, the law does not seem to have been very well observed and Charles II had to rule that "in all the streets no signboard shall hang across, but that the sign shall be fixed against the balconies or some convenient part of the side of the house."

This did not stop the erection of the greatest signboard of all time, outside the *White Hart* at Scole in Norfolk. "I came to Scaole, where there is a very handsome inne, and the noblest sygnpost in England, about and upon which are carved a great many stories as of Charon and Cerberus, Actaeon and Diana and many others: the sign itself is a White Hart which hanges downe carved in a stately wreath," wrote Sir Thomas Browne in 1663. This must have been an amazing work for it was said to have cost over a thousand pounds in those days, which would have purchased several fair taverns. It was taken down in 1795 and the various figures and carvings have simply disappeared. Several efforts have been made to trace them, but without success.

Again in 1719 a French visitor, Misson, commented "Out of London and particularly in the villages, the signs of inns are suspended in the middle of a great wooden portal, which may be looked upon as a kind of triumphal arch to the honour of Bacchus." However, this is looking ahead.

It was in Elizabeth's time that the Grand Tour started.

"There was always sent forth into several parts beyond the seas," wrote Bacon, "some young men of whom good hopes were conceived to be trained up and made fit for public employments and to learn the languages. This was the charge of the Queen, which was not much; for they travelled, but as private gentlemen and as by their industry their deserts did appear, so were they further employed or rewarded".

There were no passports at that time but travellers could not simply leave the country as they wished. They had to obtain a licence to do so. There was nothing new in this. Richard II had laid it down that not only did pilgrims going abroad have to get a licence, but he also stipulated the particular ports from which they had to sail.

Elizabeth's Treasurer, Lord Burghley, was the official empowered to issue licences to the young men off on the Grand Tour and he was opposed to the whole idea, advising fathers not to allow their sons to travel "if by so doing they get a few broken languages that shall profit them nothing more than to have one meat served in divers dishes". Eventually, Burghley got to the stage where he cross-examined applicants on their knowledge of their own country. If he was not satisfied he told them to go off and see England first.

No doubt his attitude was due to his own son's record abroad. The lad had been duly sent off with a tutor and a lot of good advice but ignored both. Even the English Ambassador in Paris could not control him. By the time Burghley could take any action he found the young sprig on the point of eloping with a maiden of noble family who was actually a nun in a convent near Paris. He had arranged to get money by selling not only his own clothes but his tutor's too. Travel certainly broadens the mind but Lord Burghley never seemed to have the same enthusiasm after this.

Young nobility might still often stay with friends and relatives but more and more the need was growing for good inn accommodation for travellers, not only abroad but also in England. Indeed a constant feature of Elizabethan times is the steady improvement in general living standards. At the start of her reign it was rare to find water laid on anywhere in a dwelling; at the close the water closet had been established.*

---

* Sir John Harington deserves to be remembered for constructing the first water closet in 1596, in his house near Bath. It was an installation com-

Unfortunately on the roads there was little improvement at all.

In the old days the monks had kept the roads and bridges in the vicinity of the abbey lands in some sort of reasonable condition. However, when Henry suppressed the monasteries he made no effective alternative arrangements for care of the highway.

Generally speaking the great Roman highways were overgrown and forgotten. Travellers accepted that roads would be bad much as they accepted snow, rain or any other natural inconvenience which made travel unpleasant. Roads might not have been natural phenomena but as no man was responsible for them, they may just as well have been.

Each town was supposed to look after the roads in its locality, but it was not easy (unless the Queen was coming) to get any real work done and in any case the general standard of what was acceptable was hopelessly low. Travellers expected holes and bogs and morasses. All they asked was that the roadway should be wide enough for them to ride around the obstacles.

Originally the law required all landowners to cut down bushes and trees within two hundred feet of any road, on either side. This was to protect travellers from highwaymen who thus had more difficulty in ambushing their victims. However, it would be difficult for landowners to obey this strictly as the line of travel shifted and twisted to avoid various new obstacles. Little effort was made to provide reasonable surfaces to the roads as there was no wheeled traffic. There was no wheeled traffic because the road surfaces were so bad. The situation was perfectly straightforward.

Poor people tramped and their betters rode horses and such goods as were transported went on the backs of pack horses.

There are pictures of tiny two-wheeled carts, in the Middle Ages, but they would hardly carry more than a pack horse. Bigger wagons were eventually built, but they had to be so strong to withstand the bad roads that they had to be built like houses and did not move much faster. With wheels twelve inches wide

mended to Her Majesty for her Palace at Greenwich and "other stately houses, that are oft annoyed with such savours as where many mouths are fed, can hardly be avoided".

and dragged by at least six horses they often travelled only eight or ten miles a day. The infirm and old women might travel in them but few others. One or two wealthy people had their own carts elaborately decorated with carvings and covering, the interior with tapestry but the embroidered cushions were on wooden seats that rested over axles without any form of springing. There are records of such contraptions—Lady Clare left her eldest daughter "her great carriage with the couvertures, carpets and cushions" in 1355—and they were extraordinarily costly: up to £1,000 at a time when a cow cost less than ten shillings.

On the Continent roads generally were better than in Britain. Charlemagne had done what he could to preserve the heritage of Roman roads and the monasteries continued to take an interest in road maintenance long after the Reformation stopped this in England. Further, the climate was often less severe.

Wheeled vehicles were, therefore, more common than in Britain. The Earl of Rutland was impressed by the coaches he saw in Holland and in 1555 he had one made by Walter Rippon. Nothing like it had ever been seen before on English roads and they "put both horse and man into amazement".

Probably Elizabeth herself was amazed. She had never had a coach herself, and presumably had not seen one either. When she was crowned in 1559 there was an elaborate procession when she wore her crown and was dressed in a cloth of gold, but there was no fairy coach for her to ride in; she was carried in an open litter "trimmed to the ground with gold brocade". Earlier, Mary gorgeously dressed "with a rich baldrick of gold pearly and stones about her neck, and a rich billement of stones and great pearl on her head", had ridden to her coronation on a pony, with a courtier following carrying her train over his shoulder.

However, in 1566 Elizabeth decided to appoint Walter Rippon her coachmaker and he built her a "hollow turning coach". It looked attractive, but still was unsprung and not only uncomfortable, but even dangerous. The Queen was so badly knocked about on one journey that she had to cancel a meeting with her ministers and on another occasion she told the French

Ambassador of a journey when she had been driven too fast and could not sit down for several days after.

However, a status symbol is a status symbol and what could be more symbolic than something costing into four figures when the National Debt was only twenty thousand pounds? Men of wealth and position started to have their own coaches built. They could only be used in town but by 1600 there were enough in London to require some control in the narrow streets. In 1601 legislation was proposed to stop men riding in coaches because it would make them indolent and effeminate.

There hardly seems to have been much fear of this, however, as the roads were no better and the carriages still unsprung. Generally for both speed and comfort the Queen continued to make most of her Progresses on horseback, and her subjects usually travelled the same way. Those who did not own a horse could hire one at a posting inn, for a few pence a mile, ride about ten miles and leave the horse at a specified inn, where another would be hired.

A certain Hobson had a posting inn of this type and he always insisted that, no matter what the customer wanted only the end horse could be hired, to ensure fair rotation. Hence the phrase "Hobson's Choice".

Travel on a large scale is usually based on commerce and in any case requires a measure of financial stability. The discovery of the New World and the great hoards of gold that the Spaniards were bringing back from South America was disrupting the whole European economy although at that time nobody understood this.

Henry VIII solved his problem by seizing the rich Church revenues. Elizabeth was rescued by the greatest buccaneer of all times, Francis Drake, who temporarily adjusted the currency balance by plundering the Spanish galleons.

The result was a period of prosperity for Britain and travel flourished. The roads remained barely passable but inns improved briskly and writing in 1617 Fynes Morrison gives a clear description of what he claims was a typical one.

"As soon as a passenger comes to an inn, the servants run to him, and one takes his horse, and walks him till he is cold, then rubs him and gives him meat, yet I must say that they are not much to be trusted in this last point without the eye of the master or his servant to oversee them. Another servant gives the passenger his private chamber and kindles his fire, a third pulls off his boots and makes them clean. Then the host or hostess visits him and if he will eat with the host or at a common table with others his meal will cost him 6d. or in some places but 4d. (yet this course is less honourable and not used by Gentlemen), but if he will eat in his chamber and commands what meat he will, according to his appetite, and as much as he thinks fit for him and his company, yea the kitchen is open to him to command the meat to be dressed as he best likes. While he eats if he have any company especially he shall be offered music which he may freely take or refuse and if he be solitary the musicians will give him the good day in the morning. . . ."

This practice of having local musicians to play to guests was common at this time; Pepys mentions payments to the musicians several times.

William Harrison also wrote very enthusiastically "our inns are also very well furnished with napery, bedding and tapestry, especially with napery: for besides the linen used at the table, which is commonly washed daily, is such and so much as belongeth unto the estate and calling of the guest. Each comer is sure to lie in clean sheets, wherein no man has been lodged since they came from the laundress". He was also impressed by the excellent service, the fine plate and great variety of wines.

His standards, of course, would not be so high as ours—in his own father's time travellers were having to use derelict church buildings for shelter.

CHAPTER 5

BRITAIN AWHEEL

If ... I had no duties, and no reference to futurity, I would spend my
life in driving briskly in a post-chaise with a pretty woman.

Dr. Samuel Johnson, 1777

PROBABLY nothing was more important in the development of
the inn, and particularly the English inn, than the stage coach.
It was the logical progress from hiring a horse at regular stages—
instead hire out several horses and a coach with a number of
passengers in it. Far cheaper than each of them hiring his own
horse (and probably a guide too).*

Whether it was actually the very first we do not know, but on
the morning of 9th April, 1657, a coach set off from Chester to
travel by stages to London and the service was to continue for
the next two centuries until the railways came.

The charge was thirty-five shillings for the single journey and
the discomfort was appalling. "This travell hath soe indisposed
mee, yt I am resolved never to ride up agayne in ye Coatche"
wrote a northern parson at the time. A little later Dean Swift set
out similar views in more detail.

---

* Any stranger to a district generally had to hire a guide for there were
no sign posts and normally no such things as road maps. The old maps of
the various counties showed villages, hills, churches, forests, rivers, castles,
sea with ships, fish, sea-monsters and Saxton's map showed, off the coast of
Anglesey, Neptune being familiar with a fleshy two legged mermaid. However, none of them showed roads at all, perhaps because roads generally
were too vague and ill-defined to merit recording. Saxton's map dated 1575,
of the Middlesex area, which of course includes London, does not even show
the Great North Road nor any of the other old Roman roads.

Roused from sound sleep—thrice called—at length I rise,
Yawning, stretch out my arm, half close my eyes;
By steps and lanthorn enter the machine,
And take my place—how cordially!—between
Two aged matrons of excessive bulk,
To mend the matter, too, of meaner folk;
While in like mood, jammed in on t'other side,
A bullying captain and a fair one ride,
Foolish as fair, and in whose lap a boy—
Our plague eternal, but her only joy.
At last, the glorious number to complete,
Steps in my landlord for that bodkind seat;
When soon, by every hillock, rut and stone,
Into each other's face by turns we're thrown.
This grandam scolds, that coughs the captain swears,
The fair one screams and has a thousand fears;
While our plump landlord, trained in other lore,
Slumbers at ease nor yet ashamed to snore . . .
Sweet company! Next time, I do protest, sir,
I'd walk to Dublin ere I'd ride to Chester.

At first the pace set was too fast. London was reached in four days, but as experience developed (and roads did not) the speed was cut and finally it was settled as a six-day journey.

When one considers what this means—that for a week the traveller was cooped up as Swift describes, unable to read or even to see much of the passing scene, from dawn until after dark—it was a wonder that the service survived its first venture.

But of course the traveller then had only the alternative of either a coach of his own, or a horse, or walking. So the stage coach succeeded and soon there were services to St. Albans and Coventry.

A service would usually be tried out in the summer and as demand built up it would extend until it was running through the year and naturally it was winter weather that made travel especially arduous. As Herman Schreiber comments: "In the Tudor period most English roads were rendered impassable by a mere downpour of rain." This condition continued a long time after the Tudor period. A century later Ralph Thoresby rode out to Ware ". . . and had some showers, which raised the washes upon the road to that height that passengers from London that were upon the road swam, and a poor higgler was drowned, which prevented our travelling for many hours, yet towards the evening adventured with some country people, who conducted us . . .

"So . . . we missed the deepest of the Wash at Cheshunt, though we rode to the saddle-skirts for a considerable way, but got safe to Waltham Cross, where we lodged. Morning, rode by Edmunton (where we had our horses led about a mile over the deepest of the Wash) to Highgate, and thence to London. I have the greatest cause of thankfulness . . . I received no damage though the ways were very bad, the ruts deep, and the roads extremely full of water, which rendered my circumstances (when meeting the loaded waggons in very inconvenient places) not only melancholy, but really very dangerous."

Abroad, the situation was generally little better. On 26th April, 1681, Louis XIV left Versailles to travel 160 miles to Bourbon l'Archambault. For weeks before, special efforts were made to prepare the road for him with the worst parts filled in with faggots, ditches cleared and the like. Thanks to this care he arrived at the watering place on 5th May—an average speed of sixteen miles a day.

Although they were the main problems, bad roads were not the only concern in winter. Apart from putting straw on the floor, there was no way in which a coach could be heated and outside passengers, like the coachmen themselves, were protected only by what they wore. In March 1812 there is a newspaper report of an event evidently as common as a motor accident nowadays. "On the arrival of the Bath coach . . . it was found that two passengers had been frozen to death and that a third man was dying."

Well might the Litany* have a special prayer for travellers. When a citizen of consequence announced his intention to travel any distance his church held a day of prayer as a matter of course and similarly nobody set off on a journey without making his

---

* Even to this day it will be seen that in the Litany travellers still have pride of place over the sick, women in labour and captives in prison.

will. This was the reality of travel before the nineteenth century. According to Schreiber in his *The History of Roads*

". . . the traveller had only one consolation: the famous English inn. The more inclement the weather and the worse the roads, the more popular the inns. When one reads the paeans of praise from travellers who had been welcomed at some inn or other with a glass of hot grog, one realizes how different England was from Italy. Whereas in the cold and rainy North the inn was a place of refuge, in the warm South it was a den of vice.

"The English roads blended so completely into the landscape that even the most detailed travel-guides were of comparatively little use . . . a foreigner was compelled to take a guide, as if he was crossing a desert or high mountains. The inns, however, flourished if only because once the traveller reached one, he was loath to leave it. The George at Glastonbury, the Pilgrim Hostel at Battle, the hostel of Godbegot at Winchester have remained famous for more than five hundred years, up to the present time."

Well, perhaps Dr. Schreiber, a German, is a little envious. Certainly at that time German roads were no better. In 1571 a hole was worn in the road from Marburg to Frankfurt so deep that three wine carts disappeared into it in succession and a labourer drowned in the quagmire at the bottom.

Nearly two centuries later Boswell notes on 27th October, 1764: "At one I set out for Frankfurt. The wagon was covered with leather, but it was a monstrous machine. One could see nothing from its little openings for it had no glasses. It jolted most horridly and as it was constructed with iron bars; when I attempted to sleep, I received most severe raps and was really in danger of having my head broke. In short, it was a trying machine, worse than my good friends the open post-wagons for upon them I could see the country, feed on the fresh air, and sleep like a mariner on the top of a mast.

". . . I had with me in the wagon a French servant, a blackguard, impudent dog. Yet at night I supped with him and my servant. Such is my hardy plan on my German travels. I also lay down with them on the straw. It was terrible. The heat of an iron stove rendered the straw musty and the air hot, and this, joined to the breaths of a good many people by no means of the most clean race rendered the room most abominable. I could not sleep. One sad circumstance in the Stube, or common room of a German inn, is being obliged to sleep with a tallow candle or a coarse lamp burning. I had recourse to the stableman and got a place in the hayloft where I slept sound though cold."

Half a century later the position had not improved. On 18th November, 1809, an enthusiastic traveller, von Eichendorff, set off for Berlin, with a friend. After a long and hectic boat journey they reached a country inn where they could get a stage coach in the morning and

". . . finally about eight o'clock stretched out on the straw, on which we spent a dreadful, sleepless night. For to begin with we were wakened by the discordant singing of Protestant hymns at the family's evening service (the innkeeper's wife in her nightdress) and the children spent the rest of the night crying.

"After cats, a whole family of hens, etc., had walked over me, I arose a little refreshed and towards nine o'clock we set off . . . some time after seven in the evening, in bright moonlight, we finally arrived at Frankfurt-an-der-Oder, half dead from frost, hunger, thirst and bruised ribs and put up at the good Golden Lion inn just outside the town . . . for the first time for almost fourteen days we undressed and went to bed."

He eventually did reach Berlin, being stopped on the outskirts at a toll bar, where the toll inspector was so drunk that he could not stand up and they had to carry all the baggage into his house so he could check it sitting down.

And yet France must have been in an even poorer state, for when Monsieur Michel de Montaigne visited southern Germany in 1580 he was favourably impressed by the inns there, which he thought not cheap but clean, and the food plentiful and excellent. This was not because he was uncritical. He complained repeatedly of some things ". . . we attended the splendid wedding of the rich and ugly daughter of a local citizen with a manager of the firm of Pugger in Venice. We did not see a single beautiful woman. . . ."

Until long after Napoleon laid out his excellent road system,

French inns, now world famous for their general excellence, were notorious both for the poor quality of the food and the high quality of the vermin. Few would claim that the native Frenchman is instinctively hospitable, as are, say, the Greek islanders, proud to be called *Philokseni*—guest-lovers, or the Andalusians —"Enter, my home is your home". The French inns became so good (they are perhaps beginning to fall off now) because the French themselves had such high standards in food and drink, in a rich country where supplies are plentiful.

However, in Napoleon's time it was English hostelries that were renowned throughout the world and this was due to the volume of traffic following the success of the stage coach. In Scotland the lack of roads held back this development. Whilst the English coaches were clipping along to nine and ten miles per hour schedules the Edinburgh to Selkirk carrier was taking a fortnight for the thirty-eight mile journey. The first coach service between Glasgow and Edinburgh did not start until 1750 and then ran only in the summer. Scottish coaching was a century behind England and their inns the same. These consisted of stabling and carriage sheds on the ground floor with a dormitory-eating place above. Arnot writing in 1779 calls them "mean buildings: their apartments dirty and dismal ... a stranger will, perhaps, be shocked with the novelty of being shown in by a dirty sunburned wench, without shoes or stockings."

Writing in 1800 the Hon. Mrs. Murray found Hawick, a stage on the Edinburgh road, to be sadly deficient. "At Hawick you must sleep, as there is no place between that and Edinburgh where you can possibly pass a night with any degree of comfort. I would advise you even to get early to Hawick, lest other travellers should be there before you: there is but one sitting room at Hawick and only one tolerable bed-chamber, with two beds." A sadly different picture from the hustle and rush of the coaching inns a couple of hundred miles south.

The next step was the mail coach. The Post Office itself had started about 1635 the private persons' (as opposed to official) mail being carried by post-boys at a cost of 2d. a letter up to eight miles and 6d. for anywhere in England, which the recipient, not the sender, had to pay.

The post-boys—usually old men mounted on any sort of a horse they could get hold of—were very unsatisfactory. They were slow, unreliable and generally suspected of being in league with local highwaymen who held them up with distressing frequency.

By 1780 the stage coach services were reliable and were running to tight time schedules (there were around a hundred vehicles on the road each day between the main cities) whilst the mail was still being carried haphazardly by post-boys as it had been a century and a half before. This was obviously absurd, but the authorities were very conservative and it was with great difficulty that Mr. Palmer persuaded the Postmaster General to let him carry the mails to Bristol in a stage coach with an armed guard protecting it. The first mail arrived in fifteen hours instead of the minimum of fifty that the post-boys took, and the service was an unqualified success. Soon every city in the country was demanding service by Mr. Palmer's mail coaches.

What was immediately necessary now was a better highway system. Roads were still regarded as little better than a natural phenomenon—nobody's special responsibility. A miller in Crieff dug a clay pit in the middle of the road. As might have been expected a stranger on horse-back fell into it in the middle of the night and was killed. The miller was prosecuted but acquitted —there was nowhere else near by where he could get clay and there was no law to stop him getting it out of the highway.

Turnpike Acts had been passed to give somebody a direct interest in improving the roads. Trustees were made responsible for a stretch of road and in return were allowed to charge a toll on all travellers. At first the tolls were more obvious than any improvement.

However, once Palmer with his mail coaches had shown what improvements could be made in old systems the atmosphere changed and in eight years over three hundred Acts were introduced for the construction of various bridges and roads.

The great engineer in charge of this construction was Thomas

Telford—a shepherd's son who built over fifteen hundred bridges and ten thousand miles of canals and roads. However, he never managed to leave a good solid surface for wheeled traffic and it was a Scot, Macadam,* who realized that wheeled traffic scattered the pebbles and natural stones with which Telford surfaced his roads.

After a lot of experiments Macadam settled for a surface made by chipping boulders into little angular stones, each of which had to be small enough for the stone breaker to put into his mouth. These rough stone chips, instead of being scattered were bedded down by wheeled traffic and at long last Britain had a road system as good as it had been in Roman times.

Now the only limit to the speed of coaches was the strength of the horses themselves. What the horses could manage the passengers had to put up with. Lord Campbell, an early and enthusiastic traveller, tells how at first it was thought that "the marvellous velocity of nearly seven miles an hour" over a long period would be "highly dangerous to the head, independent of all perils of a turnover. Stories were told (about the London–Edinburgh stage) of men and women, who, having reached Lon-

---

* He was actually of the MacGregor clan, but few people can have had better reason than he to change his name. In 1603 a law was passed making it an offence punishable by death to bear the name MacGregor, and it was still in force over two centuries later.

This was the last attempt at genocide in the British Isles and stems from ancient clan disputes. In 1563 the Laird of Glenorchy beheaded the leader of the MacGregors in front of his wife and heard her cry out that only by drinking a cup of her husband's blood could she endure her terrible grief. These were brutal times—the standard execution method at Inverary was to tear off a malefactor's arm from its socket, impale it on a pike and then hang him. Perhaps the beheaded MacGregor got off lightly.

However, his clan did not and fearsome laws were passed at the behest of the Earl of Argyle calling for the branding and transportation of Mac-Gregor women. The men were at anybody's mercy and an outlaw could earn a pardon by appearing before the justices with the severed head of a MacGregor.

Mac means "son of"—e.g. MacDonald is the son of Donald.

One of the unhappy clan changed his name to Macadam reasoning that all men are descended from Adam and so he should have no dispute about name with any clan in the future.

Had this name not been changed we might, perhaps, refer today, not to tarmacadam, but to tarmacgregor roads. (In fact Macadam never saw pitch used on his roads—until the days of motor traffic there was little need for it. He died before even the steam roller was invented).

don with such celerity, died suddenly of an affection of the brain. My friends and family were seriously alarmed for me and advised me at all events to stay a day at York to recruit myself."

It is unlikely that any present-day traveller would be prepared, as Lord Campbell was, to sit in a coach for sixty hours travelling day and night with the very briefest of stops for meals.

Because nowadays we think of horse travel as slow we picture the stage coach era as a time of leisurely travel. Far from it! The Holyhead Mail, for example, took just twenty-six hours from London. In that time it had not only covered two hundred and sixty-one miles, but there had been twenty-seven changes of horses and just forty minutes in all allowed for meals. The London to Exeter mail left London at 5 a.m. and travelled the one hundred and seventy-six miles by 10 p.m. after twenty changes. On the fast runs the coach, with post horn blowing a warning, arrived at the stage timed to the minute (half a minute on the Brighton run) where a fresh team of horses was standing ready and the changeover was completed in forty to fifty seconds.

The stage coach cracking along with its four or six fine horses is undoubtedly colourful and glamorous. So is a ship in full sail. There was little that was leisurely or easy about running either of them.

The guards on the mail coaches were duty bound to get the mail through no matter what happened. If the coach got bogged down the guard had to leave it and carry the mail on foot. A coach on the Oxford to Gloucester run broke down in Cirencester and John Jelfs, the guard, tramped the remaining seventeen miles with the mail bags on his back, through snow and floods. He was rewarded with a bonus of five shillings in his pay packet.

When the London to Chester mail was caught in a flood the guard spent four hours in the icy water rescuing passengers, repairing the coach and getting it out. There was a severe frost and he travelled then wet and frozen for hours until they reached London. The passengers were so appreciative that they commended him to the Postmaster General. He was rewarded with half a guinea but a shilling was deducted because the mail was late.

In normal course the mail coach was considered superior to the stage. It cost more, stopped at the best inns and was more reliable. It had absolute right of way on the road and did not even stop to pay tolls.

De Quincey wrote fondly of mail coach travel and tells how he helped break down an ancient snobbery. Up to 1805, the year of Trafalgar, it was generally accepted that the "quality" had the four inside seats and the three outside seats were occupied by inferior beings.

"What words, then, could express the horror, and the sense of treason, in that case, which had happened, where all three outsides (the trinity of Pariahs) made a vain attempt to sit down at the same breakfast-table or dinner-table with the consecrated four? I, myself, witnessed such an attempt; and on that occasion a benevolent old gentleman endeavoured to soothe his three holy associates, by suggesting that, if the outsides were indicted for this criminal attempt at the next assizes, the court would regard it as a case of lunacy, or delirium tremens, rather than of treason. England owes much of her grandeur to the depth of the aristocratic element in her social composition, when pulling against her strong democracy. I am not the man to laugh at it. But sometimes, undoubtedly, it expresses itself in comic shapes. The course taken with the infatuated outsiders in the particular attempt which I have noticed, was, that the waiter beckoning them away from the privileged salle-a-manger, sang out, 'This way, my good men,' and then enticed these good men away to the kitchen. But that plan has not always answered. Sometimes, though rarely, cases occur where the intruders, being stronger than usual or more vicious than usual, resolutely refused to budge, and so far carried their point, as to have a separate table arranged for themselves in a corner of the general room."

De Quincey goes on to tell how he and like-minded undergraduates altered the public attitude to the coach by travelling outside for preference. "The air, the freedom of prospect, the proximity to the horses, the elevation of seat—these were what we required; but, above all, the certain anticipation of purchasing occasional opportunities of driving."

To prove that theirs was the natural choice he tells how George III had sent a personal gift of a stage coach to the Emperor of China who had no idea what it was or how it was used. The cabinet met, worked out the general idea of the thing and the Emperor rode round Peking in his glory, sitting in the coachman's seat, whilst the coachman sat inside and put the reins through the window.

Originally it cost twice as much to travel inside as it did on top so it was taken for granted that anybody travelling outside was only there because he could not afford anything better. One had to be a "toff", patently with money—as Oxford undergraduates were in those days—to flout convention. In England, then, a man had his place in the scheme of things and he lived accordingly and travelled accordingly.

In the cities where inns were numerous there were sharp distinctions between the classes of travellers accommodated. Gentlemen in their own carriages or on horseback did not stay in inns that catered for stage coaches. The sign that we see outside public houses today "No coaches" was to be seen on the best London hotels over two centuries ago. The stage coach inns had nothing to do with the poorer travellers in the wagons, and the man tramping on foot had real difficulty getting a half-decent bed at all.

In rural situations where one inn had to serve all travellers there was the same sharp distinction in the treatment meted out. Those who made the grade ate in the dining-room or their own sitting-room. The rest had to go into the kitchen. Carl Moritz was a German clergyman who visited England and gave a fair description of a typical kitchen.

"The chimney in this kitchen, where they were roasting and boiling, seemed to be taken off from the rest of the room, and enclosed by a wooden partition. The rest of the apartment was made use of as a sitting and eating room. All around on the sides were shelves with pewter dishes and plates and the ceiling was well stored with provisions of various kinds, such as sugarloaves, black puddings, hams, sausages, flitches of bacon, etc. While I was eating a post-chaise drove up: and in a moment both the folding doors were thrown open and the whole house set in motion, in order to receive, with all due respect, these guests, who, no doubt were supposed to be persons of consequence. . . ."

They would certainly expect to be treated as persons of consequence. Smollett illustrates this in his account of Roderick Random travelling on a wagon to London and stopping at the normal inn where dinner was booked.

". . . while we were about to sit down to dinner, the innkeeper came and told us that three gentlemen, just arrived, had ordered the victuals to be carried to their apartment, although he had informed them that they were bespoke by the passengers in the wagon. To which information they had replied, 'The passengers in the wagon might be damned—their betters must be served before them—they supposed it would be no hardship on such travellers to dine upon bread and cheese for one day.' This was a terrible disappointment to us all. . . ."

We have a similar attitude in one of Fielding's characters, Mrs. Abigail, who, for certain involved reasons, had to eat in the kitchen (as poorer travellers invariably did). She demanded of the post boys:

"Why they were not in the stable with their horses. 'If I must eat my hard fare here, madam," cried she to the landlady, 'I beg the kitchen may be kept clear, that I may not be surrounded with all the blackguards in town: as for you, sir', says she to Partridge, 'you look somewhat like a gentleman, and may sit still if you please: I don't desire to disturb anybody but mob.' "

It was necessary to have money in your pocket to throw your weight about like this. The stage from Edinburgh to London originally cost £4 but as the service speeded up the prices rose and in 1800 the cost was £7. When Palmer's mail coach started the charge was £10 and another £5 had to be allowed for meals and tips. (There was no overnight stop—the mails raced down the length of the country in sixty hours practically non-stop. If this was too exhausting then the stage coach cost less but more had to be allowed for charges at the inns overnight.)

Inns were so busy and the roads so full not particularly because the number of travellers was large but because any journey took

(*Above*) THE GRITTI PALACE HOTEL *at the edge of the ocean. In Venice all hotels really are only a stone's throw from the sea.* (*Below*) GRAND HOTEL, TANGIER *on the edge of the desert. In Morocco the sun is the enemy and the architect schemes to keep it out. In the shade inside is a larged tiled courtyard that is always cool and fresh.*

(*Above*) *There really is a* WHITE HORSE INN. *In fact there are plenty around Austria and Germany but this, on the Wolfgangsee, is the original. The authentic original, that is.* (*Below*) *In both Spain and Portugal where ordinary facilities are lacking, the State provides hotels (*paradores *in Spain,* pousadas *in Portugal). In Portugal there are also similar privately owned* estalagens *or hostels. This is the Albatross at Cascais, the most expensive* estalagem *in Portugal, yet always booked for months in advance.*

so long. Now we travel from London to Edinburgh in less than a day, eating our meals, if we fly or go by train, without interrupting the journey. Two or three centuries ago the journey took a week, at least, with a couple of stops a day for meals and six or seven overnight stops. No wonder inns began to spring up on every likely road.

In these the poorer traveller ate with the landlord and his family in the kitchen—the "ordinary" meal at a cost of sixpence or so. Anything especially ordered cost more, of course—à la carte instead of what the French call table d'hote and what we for centuries called "the ordinary".

One of the features of travel in earlier days was the variety of local food. Pork pie was found at its prime around Melton Mowbray, not wrapped in plastic and tasting the same from Bristol to Braemar. A Cornish pasty was a Cornish pasty and Devonshire served its junket as Cambridge its brawn, Banbury its cheese and so on. Eating was good at a time when the countryside swarmed with game and rivers were full of fish instead of industrial wastes.

All inns of any pretensions had rooms for the "quality" who ate alone, ordering what they pleased and were free to visit the kitchen to see it prepared properly.

This practice of dining in private lingered on into the last century. Thomas Burke quotes an American visitor in 1871:

"One is made exceedingly comfortable at a first-class English hotel, but there is a stiffness about it which is not oft to be found in the best American or Continental hotels. . . . Seldom is there a public table; and if the party comprise ladies, one is forced even if staying for a single day, to take a private parlour. But I am quite converted to the English private parlour. After a long day's journey in heat and dust, struggling on with an eager and vexed human current, to be ushered into one's own room, quiet as a room at home, furnished often with books and every luxury and comfort, this goes some way towards recompensing the traveller for the exclusiveness of the thing. He is, it is true, entirely isolated. If his dearest friend were dying in the next room, he would not find it out, for seldom is there a registry-book kept in an English hotel. And one rarely risks a question to the dignified and taciturn waiter, with gravity and white cravat enough to be the Dean of Westminster."

At that time in a first-class hotel—the new Bath Hotel at Matlock, say—full board cost 5s. 6d. a day.

Normally the innkeeper considered it his duty to be a real host to his guests, especially the quality, acting as a guide around the town, introducing them to local people and then entertaining them in his inn. Pepys describes such visits in his Diary. Further, in the better inns the landlord asked his visitors to stay free as his guests over the Sabbath, and he became literally their host.

One of the oddest examples of free hospitality is described by John Taylor, a Thames waterman who became unemployed with the spread of hackney carriages. He tramped to Scotland and wrote of it in *The Pennyles Pilgrimage*.

At Cockburnspath in Scotland he:

"Lodged at an inn the like of which, I dare say, is not in any of his Majesty's dominions. And for to show my thankfulness to Master William Arnot and his wife, the owners thereof, I must explain their bountiful entertainment of guests, which is this. Suppose ten, fifteen or twenty men and horses come to lodge at their house, the men shall have flesh, tame and wild fowl, fish with all variety of good cheer, good lodging and welcome: and the horses shall want neither hay nor provender, and at the morning at their departure, the reckoning is just nothing. This is the worthy gentleman's use, his chief delight being only to give strangers entertainment gratis."

Innkeepers like Mr. Arnot were as rare then as they are today. Most people had quite a different opinion of the innkeeper and especially the staff. Writing in the sixteenth century, about highwaymen, William Harrison said:

"Seldom also are they or any other wayfaring men robbed, without the consent of the Chamberlain, tapster or ostler where they bait and lie, who feeling at their alighting whether their capcases or budgets be of any weight or not, by taking them down from their saddles, or otherwise see their store in drawing of their purses, do by and by give intimation to someone or other attendant daily in the yard or house, or dwelling hard by, upon such watches, whether the prey be worth the following or no. If it be for their turn, then the gentleman peradventure is asked which way he travelleth, and whether it please him to have another guest to bear him company at supper who rideth the same way in the morning that he doth. And thus . . . the cheat is half wrought."

In these high speed days of instant death or maiming on the road we tend to look back to earlier travel hazards with a certain nostalgia. At least in those times a man was offered the choice of his money or his life, not just smashed to pulp for an instant's carelessness.

At the time popular opinion was a little different and the romance we attach today to Robin Hood or Dick Turpin was not so obvious then. Do we regard as romantic the gangs who hi-jack lorry loads of whisky or cigarettes on our highways today? Highway thieves of one sort or another have been a scourge since the dawn of time. Originally they operated in large bands as Robin Hood was supposed to have done. It was not until pistols had reached a fair stage of development that the individual highwayman like Turpin could hold up a coachful of people. At first robbers had to rely on weight of numbers and many of the bands were enormous.

These were often rebels against a society that had made life intolerable for the underdog. Robin Hood did not become a legend because he robbed the rich to give to the poor (the poor could rob the rich themselves thank you) but as a symbol of the little man fighting back against the aristocracy and the nobility of the Church.*

In the early days the safest course was for the travellers or pilgrims to outnumber any possible robber band by travelling in a sort of convoy system. Men gathered together in the inns

* The Roman empire had a similar character in the third century A.D. Felix Bulla had a force of six hundred under his control and for two years he commanded a section of the Via Appia and nobody passed without paying him toll. Eventually a very large army contingent had to be despatched to deal with him. The commander opened proceedings by sending a centurion to Bulla to negotiate. The latter shaved his head and returned him with the message "Tell your masters they should look after their slaves better, then they will not come to me and become robbers."

around the town gates as Chaucer's Canterbury pilgrims did at the Tabard, and sallied forth in a large group.

The lone traveller tempted fate as we see in the case of Chaucer himself. At one time when he was the King's Clerk of the Works he set out from London to pay some bills at Eltham Palace. He carried with him £10, a very substantial sum in the fourteenth century. On the road four men stopped him and took the money and his horse. He walked back to London got a fresh horse, drew another £10 and set off again. At about the same point the same gang of four relieved him again of his horse and cash. Well might he have murmured "It hath been one of those days", as he plodded back into London once more.

As the traffic on the roads increased and the design of the pistol ("the old equalizer" as Damon Runyon so rightly describes it) improved, highway robbery became easier and a more individual occupation. It was not even necessary to have a horse to start in business. The *Gentleman's Magazine* reported in 1740:

"The Bristol mail from London was robbed a little beyond Knightsbridge by a man on foot who took the Bath and Bristol bags and, mounting the post-boy's horse, rode off towards London."

Even to go as a pauper, so that a thief would find nothing to steal, was not always the answer. A character who called himself the "Night Prince" operated around Paris in 1736 and he actually posted notices in the city itself threatening mayhem to anybody who ventured on to "his" roads after 10 p.m. without adequate ready cash—one hundred and twenty livres or valuables to that amount, or from artisans a quarter of this.

In 1751 travel around Naples became impossible and the King then sent out special patrols each comprising a hundred armed men, together with an executioner and a priest, but such effective measures were rare.

In fact, incredible as it may seem, two English "gentlemen of the road" tried to put their operations on some sort of a legal footing. They had a deed drawn up by lawyers and duly witnessed whereby they agreed to share their "earnings" equally. One of them, Everitt, later sued his partner, Williams, for defrauding him and the court actually made him an award. Williams, however, appealed to a higher court. There the judge had enough sense to see that a mockery was being made of the law and all concerned, including the lawyers, were punished.

Men of every walk of life became highwaymen—even women. There was a report of a case heard in August 1728 in Cork where a preacher's wife was imprisoned.

"She had for some years consorted with thieves unbeknown to her husband, in that these same thieves came frequently to the house in women's clothes, purporting to be her relations. From time to time she took a few of these relations to bed with her, leaving the poor husband to sleep on the sofa. She was in the habit of going out with the band dressed in a man's clothes, to rob on the road and she was caught in these clothes with her comrades. Following this the husband was murdered in his house by some of the band, to prevent him from betraying one or other of them."

Then, as the roads improved, the heyday of the highwayman was over. The last few lingered around Wetherby but the gent of the road had to have quiet and privacy for his operations. Once traffic became brisk his days were numbered.

And traffic did become brisk. By 1825 it was estimated that 10,000 people a day were using the mail coaches alone. Seventy coaches a day ran between London and Bath, raising a trail of dust the length of the Mall. Pumps were sunk every two miles so that the road could be kept watered in dry weather. There were about 4,000 mail and stage coaches on the road. In London there were over 3,000 inns and these had to develop to cope not merely with the travellers themselves but all the ancillary services, stabling, maintenance and staffing that the stage or mail services involved.

At Cheltenham twenty-three passenger services operated from the *Royal*. Apart from the inn side there were booking offices, luggage rooms, etc., just as a railway station has today.

The first change out of London on the West road was at Hounslow where 2,500 horses were stabled. These were split among several inns, but it was not uncommon for a busy posting house to stable 600 and 700 horses. It was reckoned that they cost £2 a week each to keep so it can be seen that the turnover would be substantial even today. All told it was estimated that about 150,000 horses were kept at the various stages.

Then in 1825 the first steam passenger railway in the world was opened; from Darlington to Stockton of all places. Five years later the Liverpool–Manchester line carried almost half a million passengers and already some mails were going by rail. In another ten years America had 178 lines covering 3,000 miles. Steam had come to push the stage coach into history.

At first the coachmen tried to compete and raised speeds. One route retimed its services to 12 m.p.h. and seven horses died with ruptured blood vessels in three weeks. Lungs could not match boilers and in the end the coaches on a route finished as soon as a railway opened.

It was an unmitigated disaster to the coachmen, the innkeepers, the ostlers, the turnpike trusts and hundreds of villages that had been on the main roads. Within decades important bustling posting villages became forgotten hamlets with gaunt empty inns struggling on by serving the odd hunt supper. Birch Reynardson wrote sadly of "the great rambling, half-aired, half-appointed inn; waiter acting boots, boots acting post-boy or maybe all three; and cook acting chambermaid, barmaid, and all."

Now it was that travellers began to recall the glories of the old coaching days. Dickens, Disraeli, De Quincey, Cobbett and a dozen others began to rhapsodize over the romance of the High-flyer, the Tantivy, the Tally-ho. When the new railway hotels went up travellers found they were being accommodated, it seemed, on a wholesale basis instead of as individuals. A great cry went up for those dreamlike coaching inns of old.

Everybody knows that Dickens despite soggy, foggy statistics created the crisp white Christmas we see on our Christmas cards. It is not so readily realized that the common Christmas card coaching scene of good cheer was equally an invention of his.

The reality of which men wrote at the time was a little different.

"The usual coach dinner—a coarse fat leg of mutton, roasted

to cinder, a huge joint of boiled beef, underdone, and gritty cabbage," said one contemporary writer.

Surtees was a worthy trencherman and he had no love of a coach dinner. He described one in a Jorrocks sketch in the *New Sporting Magazine.*

"Our travellers had been driven through the passage into a little, dark, dingy room at the back of the house, with a dirty, rain-bespattered window, looking against a whitewashed blank wall. The table, which was covered with a thrice-used cloth, was set out with lumps of bread, knives and two three-pronged forks laid alternately. Altogether it was anything but inviting, but coach passengers are very complacent; and on the Dover road it matters little if they are not. Coats Nos. 1, 2 and 3 are taken off in succession, for some people wear top-coats to keep out the heat; chins are released from their silken jeopardy, hats are hid in corners. Inside passengers eye outside ones with suspicion ... Presently the two dishes of pork, a couple of ducks, and a lump of half-raw, sadly mangled cold roast beef, with waxy potatoes and overgrown cabbages were scattered along the table. 'What a beastly dinner!' exclaims an inside dandy in a sable-collared frock; 'the whole place reeks with onions and vulgarity. . . .' 'Now harkee, waiter, there's the guard blowing his horn, and we have scarcely had a bite apiece,' cries Mr. Jorrocks, as that functionary sounded his instrument most energetically in the passage; 'blow me tight if I stir.' "

This agitation by the guard to get the party moving was a constant grumble. There was a flat charge of two and sixpence for dinner usually, whether you had time to eat it or not. The common opinion was that a landlord judiciously bribing the right guards could serve and reserve any joint for at least three successive sittings.

So the travellers wrote at the time. Obviously there must have been many excellent inns with fine food well served, especially off the main routes, where competition did not make speed such a dominant feature. However, there is no doubt that stage coaches and coaching inns look better on a Christmas card than they did at the time. Let us read what John Cressett had to say:

"What advantage is it to men's health to be called out of their beds into their coaches an hour before day in the morning, to be hurried in them from place to place till one, two, or three hours within night, insomuch that sitting all day in the summer-time stifled with heat and choked with dust, or in the winter-time starving or freezing with cold, or choked with filthy fogs? They are often brought to their inns by torchlight, when it is too late to sit up to get a supper, and next morning they are forced into the coach so early that they can get no breakfast ... Is it for a man's health to travel with tired jades, to be laid fast in foul ways, and forced to wade up to the knees in mire; afterwards sit in the cold till teams of horses can be sent to pull the coach out? ... Is it for a man's pleasure, or advantageous to their healths and business to travel with a mixt company that he knows not how to converse with; to be affronted by the rudeness of a surly, dogged, cursing, ill-natured coachman; necessitated to lodge or bait at the worst inns on the road, where there is no accommodation fit for gentlemen; and this merely because the owners of the inns and the coachmen are agreed together to cheat the guests?"

He felt so strongly that he published a pamphlet calling for the suppression of stage-coaches. Nobody seems to have explained to him that this was—as it was—the most romantic and glamourous way of travelling we have ever seen.

CHAPTER 6

WATERING PLACES AND RESORT HOTELS

And Noah he often said to his wife when he sat down to dine
I don't care where the water goes if it doesn't get into the wine.
G. K. Chesterton

As time passed inns did not cater only for travellers. Originally it was usually taken for granted that anybody making a journey would have accommodation available at his destination. Pilgrims stayed in their hostels whilst they completed their devotions and other journeys would generally be to visit relatives, with whom, of course, the traveller stayed. Otherwise, if for example, he came to a city like London on business or to press a lawsuit or the like and he knew nobody with whom to stay, he would find lodgings. Inns were rarely suitable for visits of this nature.

The next big step forward in commercial accommodation was at watering places and spas. Here for the first time people were residing temporarily, not for religious reasons, not for business, but simply for pleasure (and ostensibly for the good of their health).

The value of certain mineral springs in restoring health had been known from the earliest times. Long before the Romans established their empire and built a social life around their baths, Greek writers were recording a medical lore of science and superstition. "Where a spring rises or a river flows, there ought we to build altars and offer sacrifices," declared Seneca.

In England there is evidence at Bath of Celtic earthworks and excavations that long pre-dated the Roman occupation.

However, it was the Romans who really appreciated the value

of British wells. They developed both Bath and Buxton, being particularly taken by the hot springs of Bath—Salinus, a Latin writer of the third century, thought them one of the wonders of the world. "In Britain are hot springs furnished luxuriously for human use. Over these springs Minerva presides and in her temple the perpetual fire never whitens into ash, but as the flame fades, turns into rocky balls." Well, that's what he said.

After the great social life at the baths died with the departure of the Roman legions interest in the wells languished in Britain.

On the Continent, the Roman tradition lingered and there was more regard for the wells. In 1326 a Belgian ironmaster was cured by the chalybeate waters of a little spring near Liege and in gratitude he erected a shelter and welcomed other sufferers. The Walloon for "fountain" is "Spa" and this is what the little village came to be called.

It was nearly three centuries later before the word was first used in England. Then William Slingsby passing over "a rude barren moore" near Knaresborough noticed water bubbling from the ground. There was something about it that caught his attention and he tasted it. He had visited Spa in Belgium and realized that this water was similar. He built a wall around the spring (it still stands at the south-east end of the Stray) and so in due course Harrogate was born.

Dr. Timothy Bright on a visit there in 1596 described the well as "the English Spa" and so began the use of this word to describe the former holy wells.

A few years later a discovery similar to that at Harrogate was made much nearer London. Lord North was staying at Lord Abergavenny's shooting box at Eridge. Out riding one morning he noticed that a spring of water left a gleaming deposit on the ground. He was familiar with continental spas, he having fought in the Low Countries, and when he tasted this water he recognized the mineral flavour.

He and Lord Abergavenny sank wells and railed them in—the Tunbridge Wells.

Although these were much nearer to London it was not until 1630 that they were really established. Queen Henrietta was very familiar with continental spas and after the birth of Prince Charles (later Charles II) she went to Tunbridge Wells to recuperate. There was no accommodation at all for her or her retinue and tents had to be set up and timber buildings erected.*

Unfortunately the Roundheads then not only killed off any lingering religious traditions connected with the wells but at the same time the Englishman's chance of the gay social round of the continental spa also withered.

It was not until the Restoration that spa life started to develop again and once more the scene was Tunbridge Wells and Charles II the cause. This time it was his wife, Catherine of Braganza, who was the royal visitor, not recuperating from a birth but hoping for one.

"Chalybeate waters had the reputation of promoting fertility, and the alarming result of the visit was that though the Queen herself was proof against them, her ladies, apparently, were not," William Addison tells us in his *English Spas*. He goes on:

"Queen Catherine was far better housed than Queen Henrietta had been. She lodged on Mount Ephraim, in a house lent by Sir Edmund King, his Majesty's physician. Others of her retinue were accommodated in houses in the neighbourhood, while the rest encamped in tents on the common. Each morning they went down to the wells and after taking the waters chattered and laughed together under the spreading branches of the elm trees while they bought gloves and stockings at the shops, or tried their luck at the raffling booths, for the habit of raffling had been brought over from Paris and was already established at the wells. Gambling and flirting were the order of the day while each evening the entire company would assemble at the bowling green for open air dancing on the smooth dry turf . . .

"Life in the tents set up on the common was notoriously unrestrained. There had been a long war, aggravated by the repres-

* This appears to have been the last time that a reigning English monarch had to make do with such accommodation in England (ignoring the occasional emergency, as when George II and Queen Charlotte were travelling on the main road from Fulham to Hammersmith in 1739. It was then a badly rutted country road and at one point their coach overturned throwing them into the mud. Unable to go forward or get back they camped the night in the upturned coach.)

sions of Puritan rule, and now that the King was on his throne again—and the merriest King since the eighth Henry—it was only to be expected that mirth should gain on morals."

There was plenty of strong resistance from the Puritan clergy with a multitude of such sermons as "A Discourse against the fashion of spots, naked breasts and powder for the hair", by F. Hawkins (1644) or "A just and reasonable Reprehension of the enormity of naked breasts and shoulders, written by a grave and learned Papist". However, they do not appear to have met with a great deal of success and Count Anthony Hamilton in his *Memoirs of the Count de Gramont* tells us "never did Love behold his Empire so flourishing as here. Those who had been smitten before coming felt their ardour redoubled, and those who seemed the least susceptible of love lost all their austerity, and became different beings".

Unfortunately, it was another matter for the poor Queen who moved on to Bath hoping that the hot springs there would succeed where the cold waters of Tunbridge had failed.

This was the most important royal visit to Bath although it was not the first; James I's Queen, Anne of Denmark, had been there in 1616. Bath could never become really popular with London society until travel there became easier and when Catherine made her visit the use of the coach had become popular and some roads were a little better.

Bath, the Court realized, was accessible now whilst not being so near London that every scrap of scandal would get straight back. A stay at a spa thus became the predecessor of our present summer vacation. (Nobody in those days thought of going to the seaside unless they wanted to take ship somewhere.)

The spas near to the cities had the air of the old country fair. Hucksters and rogues of every sort set up their stalls while London jewellers, milliners, saddlers, booksellers and tailors opened branches at the better spas like Bath.

The social atmosphere at these resorts was greatly relaxed. Strangers spoke to each other without the formality of an introduction, a feature that was to intrigue Defoe when he visited Bath years later.

"Here you have all the liberty of conversation in the world, and anything that looks like a gentleman, has an address agreeable, and behaves with decency and good manners, may single out whom he pleases, that does not appear engaged, and may talk, rally, and be merry, and say any decent thing to them; but all this makes no acquaintance, nor is it taken so, or understood to mean so; if a gentleman desires to be more intimate and enter into any acquaintance particular, he must do it by proper application, not by ordinary meeting on the walks, for the ladies will ask no gentleman there, to go off the walk, or invite anyone to their lodgings, except it be a sort of ladies of whom I am not now speaking."

Addison illustrates this happily: "But you knew me at the Wells, my Lord," said a man of low degree on meeting a pump room acquaintance in St. James's Park.

"Then, Sir," retorted the peer, "I shall know you again—at the Wells."

A further aid to free social intercourse was the custom that developed later of wearing masks. At the evening social parade ladies not only wore masks, but often also hoods to hide themselves. Completely concealed in this way even the most shy could freely return the raillery of the young, and not so young, bucks. As might be expected a regular feature of Restoration plays is the pursuit of his own masked wife by some would-be gallant.

Further, that so many ladies were taking the water specifically to cure their infertility, must have had a foreseeable effect on many of the visitors, combined with the practice of mixed bathing and subsequent relaxation in déshabillé. (Mixed nude bathing, which had been customary had ceased before Catherine's visit.) Certainly there were those who could see nothing stimulating in this. How romantic or exciting would be a bedraggled appearance in a bath? Hammond commented that to see "rich and poor, blind and lame, diseased and sound, English and French, men and women, boys and girls, one with another peepe up in their caps, and appear so nakedly and fearfully, in their uncouth naked postures, would a little astonish and putte one in mind of the Resurrection."

Nevertheless many cynics took the view that ladies who visited the spas were not just seeking the waters. Writing much later on the subject the Abbé le Blanc said, in his *Lettres d'un Français*, that, to visit a spa, "The fair patient has had to feign illness, to win over the servants, to corrupt the doctor, to persuade an aunt, to deceive a husband, in a word to resort to all sorts of artifices to succeed. She naturally seeks compensation for all the trouble she has taken ... This is the place in all England to enjoy good health, and to turn it to account."

He is speaking of a much later period and before spa life could become popular suitable accommodation had to be provided for the visitors.

In Bath the *Saracens Head* was built in 1713 but that and a few other inns were quite unable to cope with the flood of visitors —8,000 by 1715. A sovereign or even a guinea a bed for a night was not an unusual charge at a time when the ordinary labourer kept a family for a week on much less. Nevertheless when the famous Beau Nash combined with Ralph Allen, of mail-coach fame, and the Yorkshire architect John Wood, to build the new Bath of elegant crescents and terraces, nobody contemplated anything like a resort hotel.

The wealthy simply rented houses or apartments into which they moved with their servants. Just as the man who could not afford his own carriage took a place in a stage coach, so generally did he stay at an inn if he could not afford to rent suitable lodgings.

On the Continent conditions were little better in the eighteenth century. One of the most highly recommended spas was Plombieres in the Vosges mountains but when Mme du Chatelet went to stay there with Mme de Boufflers she had to lodge in a house in which fifty other visitors were housed. She had to share her room with a dreadful old man: her bed being separated from his only by a thin curtain.

Yet Mme du Chatelet was the mistress of Voltaire, not only the most eminent man of his time, but wealthy as well. She herself was of noble birth, her husband a Grand Marshal and she could afford (or at any rate she did) to lose a fortune in a night's gambling.

Mme de Boufflers fared a little better. She was the mistress of King Stanislas of Lorraine and had a room to herself.

It was out of these conditions that a demand developed for more suitable accommodation at the spas and so grew the famous Swiss hotel tradition.

It is hard to find a time when Switzerland had not been famous for its health-giving waters. The Romans visited St. Moritz not for winter sports but for the rusty red water and through the centuries visitors forced their way every summer to the various wells. Generally they stayed with local residents for here again there were few inns. As late as 1797 a correspondent was complaining of the lack of any good inn in St. Moritz.

Eventually the resort hotel was born, largely due to the difficulties of travel before the railways came. When a family finally reached its destination the tendency was to stay for a couple of months, rather than a couple of weeks, for all the travail over the bad roads to be worthwhile.

One of the first hotels of which we have a record is the old *Hotel Interlaken*. Originally, in the fifteenth century, a hostel was built in front of the old monastery and as the years went by this was adapted and altered and then finally rebuilt in 1759.

There are a number of other establishments with very old connections, but the leading hotel at the start of Swiss tourism, as we know it today, was the *Hotel Byron* at Villeneuve near Montreux. Like many early Swiss hotels it was a large house converted to accommodate guests. It is pleasing that it was named after the poet Lord Byron, a guest there with Shelley, rather than the conqueror Napoleon, who had stopped there half a century earlier, before going on to Marengo. The *Byron* had many eminent guests including the Royal family of Greece and the Grand Duchess of Luxembourg. However, after the railway line was opened the proprietors, two brothers called Wolff, sold the hotel because business fell off. The purchaser also failed and finally the *Byron* was shut up. It is odd that the opening up of communications should have had this effect on a leading Swiss hotel but Fanny Kemble, the actress, explained this in a letter home.

"The railroad now runs all the way from Geneva to the foot of the Simplon, an easy journey of less than eight hours and nobody wants to stop halfway at Villeneuve. Then too there is really almost a continuous terrace all along the shore of the lake from Lausanne to Villeneuve of hotels like palaces, one more magnificent than another, with terraces and gardens and fountains and bands of music and luxurious apartments, and table d'hote, that it is absolutely impossible [sic] that some, if not several proprietors of such costly establishments should fail, especially as in travelling, as well as everything else, fashion directs the movements of the great majority of people. For the last few years there has been a perfect insane rush of the whole tourist world to the valley of the upper Engadine, to the almost utter forsaking of the formerly popular parts of Switzerland." However, the *Byron* did not stay closed, as Mrs. Kemble feared. It re-opened with the next swing of fashion, to flourish again.

At Zurich the *Hotel Baur Au Lac* was another important original, perhaps the first building in Switzerland to be designed from scratch specifically as a hotel. Johannes Baur, originally a baker's boy, planned it himself and it was opened in 1838. With a hundred and forty beds it was considered quite gigantic, but after only five years it had to be extended. Further expansion followed. In the end the hotel had to be practically rebuilt and the townspeople were mystified as the operation developed. When it was complete the reason for Baur's apparently odd methods became clear. The hotel was no longer facing the town, as all proper hotels did. It faced the lake; an arrangement nobody had ever contemplated before.

The Baurs became a leading hotel family and the son, Theodor, started the first professional school for hotel staff.

All this time visitors took it for granted that as the summer ended it was essential to get out of Switzerland before the snows came down and they might be trapped for the winter.

So the Swiss spent their lonely winters amid their glistening snow caps, with the hot sun sparkling out of a bright sky and wondered what sort of places their visitors hurried off to, that could be better. It was not until about the middle of the nineteenth century that the English realized that whilst Switzerland was delightful in the summer it was paradise in the winter. According to Willi Frischauer it was M. Badrutt who persuaded some English visitors to the *Palace Hotel* to stay on in St. Moritz and enjoy a Swiss winter instead of returning to the grime of Victorian London. Skating was already a European pastime, but ski-ing was something new to visitors and, of course, there soon followed the great toboggan runs. At long last winter sports had arrived and there was something for the international set to do in the winter.

The Swiss hotel tradition has long dominated the European scene, but in the early nineteenth century it was still England that led the world. Prince Puckler-Muskau a critical (and much criticized) visitor from Germany gives a detailed description of the accommodation available to those who could afford it.

The Prince had married a wealthy countess and although he was glad of her dowry it was also a genuine love-match. Unfortunately, he was obsessed by a passion to create a wonderful park as a setting for his palace in Muskau. He ran through the dowry money almost before the wedding, planting a million trees and employing an army of workmen.

He lived in the palace with his bride on credit until her father died. They expected then to inherit a further fortune, but were shocked to find that the old man had disinherited his daughter in favour of a greedy mistress. The Prince and his wife had a vast wooded estate and no money.

In those days there was only one solution to such a problem. The Prince had to divorce his well-loved wife and set off to England to find a wealthy heiress he could marry and so restore the family fortune.

During his search he wrote almost daily to his ex-wife who kept his letters. Although the Prince was popular in England and welcome at all levels of society he failed to make a suitable match, presumably because his heart was not really in fortune hunting.

Eventually he returned to his debt-ridden palace and divorced wife. She showed him the piles of letters he had sent her and which she thought could be published.

The first book *The Tour of a German Prince* was a resounding world-wide success and for the rest of his life the Prince was a wealthy best-seller writer.

The whole story is exaggerated Ruritanian musical comedy of the 1930s. Ivor Novello could have done a dozen different treatments of it. The only feature that is difficult to accept is that it is all true and did actually happen.*

Many features of English life intrigued the Prince. He wrote, for example, describing the celebrated dentist, Mr. Cartwright, who operated "in the most grandiose style. In the first place, he goes to no one, except the King: every subject male or female, must wait on him. But this is not all—you must announce yourself a week or fortnight beforehand and solicit an audience..."

One wonders what the Prince would make of today's National Health Service.

Generally, his impression of England was favourable and he wrote of it then as travellers today often write of America, as a thriving bustling land of unlimited wealth.

"What would delight you here is the extreme cleanliness of the houses, the great convenience of the furniture, and the good manners and civility of all serving people. It is true that one pays for all that appertains to luxury (for the strictly necessary is not much dearer than with us), six times as high; but then one has six times as much comfort. In the inns everything is far better and more abundant than on the Continent. The bed, for instance,

---

* The Prince owed his success to a sharp eye and a sharp pen. For instance, on the old home-entertainment when every guest "happened" to have his music with him: "That a man should advance to the piano-forte with far greater confidence than a David, strike with his forefinger the note he thinks his song should begin with, and then 'entonner', like a thunder clap (generally a note or two lower than the pitch), and sing through a long 'aria' without rest or pause, and without accompaniment of any sort, except the most wonderful distortions of face—is a thing one must have seen to believe it possible, especially in the presence of at least fifty people. Sometimes the thing is heightened by their making choice of Italian songs: and in their total ignorance of the language, roaring out words which, if they were understood by the ladies, would force them to leave the room."

which consists of several mattresses laid one upon another, is large enough to contain two or three persons; and when the curtains which hang from the square tester supported on substantial mahogany columns, are drawn around you, you find yourself as it were in a little cabinet—a room, which would be a very comfortable dwelling for a Frenchman. On your washing-table you find—not one miserable water-bottle, with a single earthen or silver jug and basin, and a long strip of towel, such as are given you in all hotels and many private houses in France and Germany; but positive tubs of handsome porcelain, in which you may plunge half your body; cocks which instantly supply you with streams of water at pleasure; half a dozen wide towels; a multitude of fine glass bottles and glasses, great and small; a large standing looking-glass, foot-baths, etc., not to mention other anonymous conveniences of the toilet, all of equal elegance.

"Everything presents itself before you in so attractive a guise that as soon as you wake you are allured by all the charms of the bath. If you want anything, the sound of your bell brings either a neatly dressed maid-servant, with a respectful curtsey, or a smart well-dressed waiter, who receives your orders in the garb and with the air of an adroit valet; instead of an uncombed lad, in a short jacket and green apron, who asks you, with a mixture of stupidity and insolence 'Was schaffen's Ihr Gnoden?' (What is it, Your Honour?), or 'Haben Sie heir Jeklingelt?' (Was it you, here, that rung?), and then runs out again without understanding properly what is wanted. Good carpets cover the floors of all the chambers; and in the brightly polished steel grate burns a cheerful fire, instead of the dirty logs or the smoky and ill-smelling stoves to be found in so many of our inns.

"If you go out, you never find a dirty staircase, nor one in which the lighting serves only to make darkness visible. Throughout the house, day and night, reign the greatest order and decency; and in some hotels every spacious set of apartments has its own staircase, so that no one comes in contact with others. At table, the guest is furnished with a corresponding profusion of white table linen and brilliantly polished table utensils; with a well-filled 'plat de menage' and an elegance of setting out which leaves nothing to wish for. The servants are always there when you want them, and yet are not intrusive: the master of the house generally makes his appearance with the first dish, and inquires whether everything is as you desire—in short the best inns afford everything that is to be found in the house of a travelled gentleman, and the attendance is perhaps more perfect and respectful. It is true the reckoning is of a-piece with the rest, and you must pay the waiters nearly as much as you would a servant of your own. In the first hotels, a waiter is not satisfied with less than two pounds a week for his own private fees. Such gifts or vales are more the order of the day in England than in any other country, and are asked with the greatest shamelessness even in the churches."

This, then, was how the wealthy could live when they travelled. This, and the good posting houses on the road were the heights which Europe achieved after centuries of slow progress. But Europe was not all the world.

CHAPTER 7

AMERICAN INNS

"Lodging and clean sheets—3s.; dirty sheets 1s."
Sign at an inn in Tarrytown,
near Hudson, New York, 1798

IF a planning expert had been asked in the seventeenth century to prescribe the best conditions for the rapid development of a hotel industry he could have summed up all his requirements in one word—America.

Americans travelled as naturally as the rest of the world stayed at home, as new territories opened up there was a constant demand for temporary housing and, generally, America had lavish supplies of good food whilst all classes had comparatively high incomes. Finally, to bring the business to a pitch of perfection there were constant fires. With appalling repetition any history of American hotels records their frequent destruction by fire. Most of the hotels now standing that were erected a century ago have probably been burned down and rebuilt at least once and more likely two or three times. Several burned down on the night they were opened.

The insurance companies were gloomy about this, but it did mean that once a hotel was established the opportunity was very likely to arise for a new and improved version to be built in its place subsequently and probably a still better successor another ten or fifteen years later.

Inn-type accommodation first appears in the New World, as far as we know, at Quebec in 1608. Champlain had built the "Habitation" there, a group of buildings primarily a fort, and this included accommodation for the traveller. Although he had to pay for his keep, it was hardly an inn.

The first real inn we can trace was apparently at Jamestown, Virginia, around 1610. It was of this place that Colonel William Byrd wrote caustically that "like true Englishmen they built a church that cost no more than fifty pounds, and a tavern that cost five hundred".

Unfortunately that is all that is recorded of this first establishment.

In what was to become New York the first building on Manhattan Island was erected in 1613, but the first permanent settlement was not made until 1626. An old map drawn in 1642 shows a tavern near the East River, not far from Bowling Green. Governor Kieft of New Netherlands, tired of having to entertain all visitors to the early New Amsterdam settlement in his own home so he had built an inn, the Staats Herberg or City Tavern for the West India Company and leased it to Philip Giraerdy for three hundred guilders "provided that only the company's liquors be sold". This Philip is thus the first landlord in the New World of whom we have a record. The building was also used as New Amsterdam's Stadt Huys or City Hall. During the Civil War it was occupied as a fortress and was shelled. This weakened it and although it became the City Hall of New York it was demolished in 1700.

In 1643 Broadway was beginning to take shape and resemble a street and another tavern was built on what is now 9–11 Broadway. By 1649 it is reported that there were seventeen "taphouses".

Outside of New York, the *Hancock Tavern* in Boston and the *Blue Anchor* in Philadelphia are the first inns of which we have any real record. Just when Hancock's tavern was established is not clear, but a public house is known to have stood on the site in 1634 with a Samuel Cole as landlord. This inn was known as Coles until John Hancock* was made Governor of Massachu-

* Hancock was one of the leading lights in the Revolution (indeed he had expected to be the first President and was so disappointed when Washington was elevated that he would not receive the new President when he stopped in Boston on his way to the Inauguration).

setts. A portrait of the new Governor was hung outside Coles and this came to be regarded as an inn sign and gradually the tavern became known as "Hancock's".

More is known of the *Blue Anchor Tavern* which stood in Front Street, Philadelphia. "In the year 1671", Mr. Glenn wrote in the *Pennsylvania Magazine of History and Biography*, "it was proposed by Captain Carr, on behalf of the townspeople of New Castle and Plantations on Delaware, to the Governor and Council, 'That ye number of Strong Drink be ascertained, That is to say, three only for ye towne and some few up Ye River, who ye officers shall think fitt and approve'." Of some few up Ye River the *Blue Anchor* became one.

When William Penn landed from the Delaware River in Philadelphia it was at the *Blue Anchor* that he was welcomed to the new state. At that time the landlord was Captain William Dare. The building had a front of sixteen feet and was thirty-six feet deep, standing on the bank of Dick Creek. There were numerous changes of tenancy subsequently and eventually it was not clear where the original inn had stood and there were two houses claiming the honour.

Wherever there was a port an inn was established and, eventually, along the high roads as well. H. Cabot Lodge commented: "the taverns were probably the most uncomfortable habitations in the province", but this was just a sparsely settled fringe of civilization in a wilderness stretching to the west.

The establishment of inns and taverns, "ordinaries" they were called in New England, spread very rapidly. The early settlers had no qualms about strong drink and the Puritan settlers took it as much for granted as anybody else that a settlement needed its ordinary.

The selectmen of the towns often met in them and at Gloucester, for example, in 1744, the annual salary of the five men chosen was $5 each the rest being taken out in tavern charges which amounted to $150. The following year the selectmen got $25 a year "and to find for themselves".

In Cambridge also the selectmen met in a tavern, usually the *Blue Anchor*. In 1769 their bill was nearly $25.

Ordination Day was surprisingly profitable. Ordination beer was brewed for the visiting ministers and there would often be an Ordination Ball. For one Hartford Ordination there is extant the tavern bill:

	£	s.	d.
To keeping Ministers		2	4
2 mugs Tody		5	10
5 Segars		3	–
1 Pint Wine		–	9
3 lodgings		9	–
3 bitters		–	9
3 breakfasts		3	6
15 Boles Punch	1	–	–
24 dinners	1	16	–
11 bottles wine	–	3	10
5 mugs flip	–	5	10
5 Boles Punch	–	6	–
3 Boles Tody	–	3	6

This bill is endorsed "all paid for except the Ministers' rum".

These early American ordinaries were always close to the meeting houses. The settlers often had long drives to the religious service and the meeting houses were never heated. In the winter, therefore, it was essential to have somewhere for travellers to thaw out before settling down for a two-hour sermon, perhaps entitled "An Arrow against Profane and Promiscuous Dancing. Drawn out of the Quiver of the Scriptures", or "The Unloveliness of Love-Locks, or a summarie Discourse proving the wearing and nourishing of a Love-Lock to be altogether unseemly and unlawful unto Christians, with some passages out of the Fathers against Face Painting".

Suitably inspired, the congregation moved back to the ordinary after the service to relax, get warm and eat a midday meal, probably brought in a saddlebag, with a glass or two of "flip". It was from this origin that there developed the practice, common in North American inns right up to the nineteenth century, of having separate dining arrangements for men and women.

Whilst the early Puritans, therefore, took it for granted that even the most Godly men had need of suitable refreshment, they were very careful to avoid any unseemly behaviour or excess. In 1645 landlords were forbidden "to suffer anyone to be drunk or drink excessively, or continue tippling above the space of half an hour in any one of their said houses under penalty of 5s. for every such offence suffered: and every person found drunk in the said houses or elsewhere shall forfeit 10s.; and for every excessive drinking he shall forfeit 3s. 4d.; for sitting idle and continuing drinking above half an hour 2s. 6d. and it is declared to be excessive drinking of wine when above half a pint of wine is allowed at any one time to one person to drink: provided that it shall be lawful for any strangers or lodgers or any person or persons in an orderly way to continue in such houses of common entertainment during meal times or upon lawful business what time these occasions shall require".

The stocks were also used as a punishment for drunkenness and when this failed to effect a cure offenders had to wear a large D—for drunkard—in scarlet on a white background.

Primarily and very sensibly the community relied for its sobriety on the good sense of the landlords. These were chosen carefully and were usually men of some standing, e.g. John Howe, land-lord of Longfellow's *Wayside Inn,* was amongst the first in the settlement to be admitted a freeman and was a selectman in 1642. In 1655 he was appointed to see to the restraining of youth on the Lord's Day.

In Ipswich, Mass., Corporal John Andrews had his licence for the *White Horse* withdrawn in 1658 because he kept his bar open after 9 a.m. and encouraged young men to drink. In his place the licence was granted to Deacon Moses Pengry. The Deacon's licence was "not to draw beer above 1d. a quart and to provide meate for men and cattell". He and other licensees were "not to sell by retail to any but men of family and of good repute nor sell any after sunsett; and that they shall be ready to give account of what liquors they sell by retail the quantity, time and to whom".

While these conditions made for sober living they were hardly conducive to the relaxation one usually expects in an inn. Nevertheless the whole life of the community naturally centred on the one place where all the citizens could forgather. It even happened in early days that church services would be held in the ordinary until a church or meeting-house was built. This happened at Goodman Mowry's tavern at Providence, Rhode Island, where Roger Williams preached for many years. Goodman Mowry was licensed in May 1655 to keep a house of entertainment and to "sett out a convenient signe at ye most perspicuous place of the said house thereby to give notice to strangers that it is a house of entertainment".

One winter morning in 1660 a young Dutchman, Clauson, was found dying on the roadside. He had been hit on the head with an axe. Mowry's inn was nearby and Clauson was carried in. Before he died he cursed his murderer and his children and grandchildren—the curse of being "marked with split chains and haunted by barberry bushes".

The deed was eventually fastened on to an Indian, Waumanitt, who was locked up in Mowry's tavern and securely guarded. This was the only prison accommodation available, but even as a temporary measure it was unsuitable. A Puritan ordinary in which church services were held was no place to confine a redskin murderer and it was determined accordingly "that the prisoner Waumanitt shall be sent down unto Newport to the Colony prison there to be kept until his tyme of triell".

Waumanitt was the first murderer ever to be apprehended in America and simply handling him posed technical problems. There was, for example, no provision for paying the expenses involved in his arrest and the town treasurer directed that the victim's property should be sold and all costs paid out of the proceeds. As Clauson had no known relatives this was perhaps not an unreasonable expedient, but it seems odd to note landlord Mowry being paid four shillings for houseroom for the prisoner out of Clauson's estate. Also to be paid was the blacksmith who charged "for irons" to bind the murderer—there being nothing in the nature of penal equipment then available.

Not only was the ordinary freely used for community purposes in this way, but equally easily a meeting house might become a tavern. This happened at Little Compton and again at Charleston, Mass. The great House at Charleston was the official residence of Governor Winthrop until 1663 when it was made a meeting house and later became the *Three Cranes* public house.

One deterrent to the development of good inns was an astonishing regulation quoted (in Dunbar's *History of Travel in America*) from Berkeley's *History of Virginia*. This stated that in the Old Dominion innkeepers were forbidden by law to charge travellers any stated amount for board and lodging. They had to accept whatever the traveller volunteered to give them.

It is hard to find any further details of this extraordinary legislation but in Colonial days "racon" taverns were common. These were private residences where travellers might be accommodated and on leaving paid "a reasonable reckoning" (raconing).

Obviously, as the country was opened up every type of accommodation might be used to house travellers. In the early days there were more inns in Pennsylvania than anywhere else because young men venturing out into unexplored Ohio, Illinois or Indiana or even farther, from the settled areas of New York and New Jersey and often Virginia, would pass through Pennsylvania. In the poorer taverns a traveller or a teamster or wagoner could drink, have supper of a kind and then stretch out on the tavern floor as near as he could get to the fire for the night. The wise would have bundles of skins with them to sleep on.

As settlements were established away from Puritanical New England there was little to stop anybody who could get a supply of liquor from building a log hut, putting up a sign "Tavern" and going out into the woods to shoot something for his wife to put into the pot (pot-luck).

There is a description of a typical inn when Chicago was a village. By the time this was written first-class inns were common in New England and many other places but it gives a fair picture of what the early traveller could expect once he left the settled areas at any period.

"It [the description of the inn] will answer for nineteen out of twenty of all we have stopped at during our journey. The outer door opens into a large dirty room full of smoke, used as a sitting room for men folks and also as a bar room, for in one corner, generally in the angle, you will see a cupboard with two or three shelves, on which are arranged in bottles the different coloured liquors. I suppose the colour is about the only difference you would have found in them; the brandy, gin and whisky generally came from one distillery, in Ohio, with the addition of burnt sugar and juniper berries to suit the taste of their customers.

"From this room you would enter the family sitting room, also used as a dining room for travellers and out of that usually a kitchen and small family bedroom. The upper storey, although sometimes divided into two rooms was often left as one, with beds arranged along the sides. Once in a while you might find a curtain drawn across the further end of the room, affording a little privacy for the female part of the occupants, but not often even that, the beds being occupied promiscuously on the first come first served principle. As for the table they set—well I suppose they did the best they could for certainly there were few dainties to be purchased that winter for love or money and the appliances for cooking were far from what they are now. In many, a pot hung over the wood fire, a frying pan and a baking pot being about all they had for culinary purposes in those days.

"Meals usually consisted of bread, butter, potatoes and fried pork; now and then you might get a few eggs but not as far west as Michigan City. Such were the accommodations travellers had to put up with in these early days. If they could find a tin wash basin and clean towel for the whole party to use, generally used standing on a bench outside the back door, they considered themselves fortunate. Nine times out of ten the beds were all occupied, or at least bespoken, but our travellers were well prepared for such occurrences, as the one-horse wagon was filled with mattresses, blankets, pillows, flocks and other articles to make a comfortable bed on the floor, which was done according to circumstances sometimes in the bar room sometimes in the dining room."

Obviously inns were not always dirty and some were well kept in the circumstances but these were certainly the exception.

One of the best descriptions we have of inns in early New England comes from the *Diary of Mme Knight*. Her parents were among the first settlers of Charlestown. In 1673, when she was only seven her father returned from three years absence at sea. Her mother met him on the steps where he gave her a hearty kiss. For this "lewd and unseemly conduct" he was promptly put in the stocks.

In due course the girl married a Richard Knight but he had disappeared from the scene in 1704. That year Mme Knight had to travel from Boston to New York in connection with some property settlement. Her husband must have been dead or abroad for no woman ever travelled alone in those days. Apparently she had no alternative; a relative accompanied her to Dedham and from there she hired guides or travelled with the post.

She wrote an excellent account of this journey and the diary was preserved in the family until 1825. It was published then and reviewers generally assumed it was a clever forgery. Libraries classed it as fiction. Later it was realized that this was an authentic picture of early New England and now it is highly prized. Reading it shows that the journey was not avoided by women because of any reason of delicacy; travel was difficult and dangerous with rivers to be crossed by swimming a horse or by canoe, and swamps and forests to be traversed without any road or even path. Her journey started on 2nd October, 1704, and eventually she reached Rye and stayed "in an ordinary which a French family kept. Here being very hungry, I desired a fricasee wch the Frenchman undertakeing, managed so contrary to my notion of Cookery, that I hastned to Bed supperless ... arriving at my apartment I found it to be a little lean-to chamber furnisht among other Rubbish with a High Bed and a Low one, a long table a Bench and a Bottomless chair. Little Miss wnt to scratch up my Kennell [mattresses were all of straw then of course] wch Russelled as if shee'd bin in the Barn among the Husks and suppose such was the contents of the Tickin—nevertheless being exceedingly weary down I laid my poor Carkes never more tired and I found my covering as scanty as my bed was hard. Anon I heard another Russelling noise in the room and called to know the matter—Little Miss said she was making a bed for the men, who when they were in bed complained that their Legges lay out of it by reason of the shortness. My poor bones complained bitterly, not being used to such lodging and so did the man who was with us and poor I made but one Grone wch was from the time I went to Bed to the time I riss wch was about three in the morning, Sitting up by the fire till Light."

When she eventually made the return journey she was feted all the way back and her "kind relations and friends" flocked to hear of her "transactions and travails". Subsequently, she travelled down to Connecticut and eventually finished up as an innkeeper herself. We have no details of the quality of her inn-keeping but she was fined in 1717 for selling liquor to Indians.

It will be seen that again we have this reference to communal sleeping which had been a feature of medieval European inns. Over a century later it was still a feature as E. A. Talbot notes.

"On entering one of these taverns and asking for a single bed you are told that your chance of getting one depends entirely on the number of travellers who may want accommodation for the night and if you obtain possession of a bed by promising to receive a companion when required, it is impossible to say what sort of a companion may come . . .

"I remember once being compelled to take a bed on these conditions, because I could not otherwise procure it. I retired early to rest and after contending a short time with my apprehension of some ineligible bed-fellow, I dropped asleep. About midnight, I was awakened by the nattering of five buxom girls, who had just entered the room and were beginning to undress themselves. Perceiving that there were only four beds in the apartment, each of which was already occupied by one person, I set it down as certain that I should have one, if not two, of these ladies. Under this impression, I raised my head, and desired to be informed which of them intended me the honour of her company. 'Don't be alarmed, sir,' cried one of them, 'we shall not trouble you nor your bed. A look is quite sufficient!'

"I suppose I must have discovered some signs of fear and

probably looked horribly enough; for the idea of three in a bed was rather a formidable affair. This, however, was the first time in my life that I owed the luxury of a single bed or any other luxury, to my looks . . . My prospect of good fortune was speedily confirmed by the sight of a large bed arranged on the floor, in which the five young ladies had composed themselves to rest."

Sleeping together in these circumstances was not generally considered immoral if for no other reason than that a woman rarely travelled alone. Mme Knight caused a commotion when she arrived at an inn unaccompanied and for many years after this a lone female would be more likely to be turned away from an inn than admitted.

Further, of course, Mme Knight was nearly forty when she undertook her journey. Nowadays a woman of forty might be regarded as just coming to the prime of life, but in the hard days of Colonial America a woman who survived to this age generally showed ample evidence of the harsh years.

Nevertheless, it would be naive to suppose that chance bed-mates did not notice their partners. Jefferson Williamson tells of a visitor to Connecticut in 1820 who was being berated for his dissipated way of life by a very respectable matron. She went on for some time and eventually he commented that in certain circumstances all people would behave in the same way. She could not imagine that she would ever behave in the same way, as he would, whatever the circumstances. "Suppose then, Madam," he replied, "that in travelling you come to an inn, where all the beds were full except two, and in one of these was a man, and in the other a woman, which would you take?—" "Why the woman's, to be sure." He nodded, "So would I."

Clearly, less than 150 years ago, bed-sharing was still taken for granted in America whereas fifty years earlier, in Europe Laurence Sterne had been surprised to have to share his room with a lady and her maidservant. "As there was no other bed-chamber in the house," he tells in *Sentimental Journey*, "the hostess without nicety led them into mine, telling them, as she ushered them in, that there was nobody in it but an English gentleman . . . there were three beds and but three people . . ."*

It was to be many years before American inns even aspired to separate beds but perhaps in a country where "bundling" was an established practice, this was not altogether surprising.

Naturally the standards of inns varied, as they do today. They were not all primitive. The *Sun Inn* of Bethlehem, Pennsylvania, was built about 1758 and housed many distinguished visitors, such as Washington, Franklin, Lafayette, as well as numerous British officers taken prisoner during the War of Independence. One of these was Lt. T. Aubrey who wrote:

"You may be sure our surprise was not a little after having been accustomed to such miserable fare at other ordinaries, to see a larder displayed with plenty of fish, fowl and game. Another matter of surprise, as we have not met with in all our travels, was excellent wines of all sorts, which to us was the most delicious treat, not having tasted any since we left Boston, for notwithstanding the splendour and elegance of several families we visited in Virginia, wine was a stranger to their tables. For every apartment a servant is appointed to attend, whose whole duty is to wait on the company belonging to it and who is as much your servant during your stay as one of your own domestics. The accommodation for horses is equal. In short, in planning the tavern they seem solely to have studied the ease, comfort and convenience of the travellers and it is built upon such an extensive scale that it can readily accommodate 160 persons."

Still more impressed by the excellence of American inns was John Lambert, an English visitor who like "all travellers of consequence, all foreigners of distinction" put up at *Gregories*.

---

* "Communal" beds are still to be found in Eastern Europe, as well as other parts of the world, even today. In his *Gates of the Wind*, Michael Carroll writes of sleeping in the house of Vangeli the Mayor of Skopelos on a Grecian island. "Upstairs in Vangeli's house there is a long seven foot wide 'shelf' stretching and filling one end of the room. This is a bed; not by any means the only bed in the room—there are three others—but certainly the most interesting one. It was covered with thin straw mattresses, cushions and bright heavy island-woven blankets. At one end of it slept Angelina and I, and at the other end two grey haired women—who came every year to help the family with the fruit and olive harvests. But there was plenty of room; the bed fifteen feet broad, had often slept, according to Alexandra, seven people at a time."

THE ALGONQUIN (*above*) *is not very large, is old fashioned and is on the wrong side Manhattan yet it is probably the most famous hotel in America. For half a century it has been the centre of New York's literary and theatrical life. Thurber, Ross, the creator of the* New Yorker, *Dorothy Parker and the rest of the Vicious Circle met here. Their legendary Round Table still exists and the Algonquin still flourishes. Below: these are renting apartments at Cap d'Ail but it is a development to be seen anywhere near the sea where one can depend on hot sun in the summer. Houses the maximum number of city dwellers who want to get away from it all as economically as possible. In the evening, when everybody sits out on their balconies, from the ground one is reminded irresistibly of the battery cages on a poultry farm.*

TO SUM UP: *From the Palace of the Past to the Latest Development. Above: in Buçaco, Portugal, the Palace Hotel once was a real palace. Now it is a superb hotel. Below: visitors go to the South for the sun. If they can depend on the sun why waste money on buildings? On a number of islands (this is at Corfu) little holiday villages of reed huts are popular with younger sun devotees—full circle?*

In Albany the Gregories had built the Tontine Coffee House in 1750, without a bar, but liquor was sold with meals.

"We had excellent accommodation at Gregory's" (he wrote) "which is equal to many of our hotels in London. At the better sort of American taverns or hotels, very excellent dinners are provided between 2 and 3 o'clock—they breakfast at 8 o'clock upon rump steak, fish, eggs and a variety of cakes with tea or coffee. The last meal is at 7 in the evening and consists of as substantial a fare as the breakfast, with the addition of cold fowl, ham, etc." This was for $1.50 or $2 a day. "Americans live in a much more luxurious manner than we do, but their meals, I think, are composed of too great a variety and of too many things to be conducive to health. Formerly, pies, puddings and cyder used to grace the breakfast table, but they are now discarded from the gentler houses and are found only in the small taverns and farm houses in the country."

As in Europe American inns made the greatest progress after the establishment of the stage coach.

In 1783 Captain Levi Pease put on the first regular stage between Boston and Hartford and so started a systematic communication between Boston and New York and became known as the Father of the Turnpike. He had a partner, Colonel Reuben Sykes, who provided most of the finance and on 20th October, 1783, Pease started from Boston and Sykes from Hartford, at 6 a.m. in "2 convenient wagons". They met midway at Spencer, swapped passengers and returned. The fare was $10, the venture was completely successful and soon the fare dropped and passengers could carry up to fourteen pounds of luggage free.

Originally, Pease operated from Shrewsbury because he could not afford the high Boston rents, but he soon prospered and bought the *Farrar Tavern* in Shrewsbury. This was very much a posting house, with a large shed for loaded wagons to stand in and another where the teamsters were served. In the side of the house, slight holes were cut, one above the other to a window on the second storey. These were just large enough for a man to hold on to and admit the toe of his boot. By this means, the men who had to leave at cockcrow or earlier could let themselves out without disturbing the rest of the household.

A French visitor was most impressed by the American posting inns. Brissot de Warville was a leading journalist who visited America and travelled by post from Boston to New York.

In the first day they travelled sixty-one miles to Spencer where he considered the inn to be good "the chambers were neat, the beds good, the sheets clean, supper passable, cider, tea punch and all for fourteen pence . . . now compare, my friend, this order of things with what you have a thousand times seen in our French taverns—chambers dirty and hideous, beds infected with bugs, those insects which Sterne calls the rightful inhabitants of taverns, if, indeed, long possession gives a right; sheets ill washed and exhaling a fetid odour; bad covering, wine adulterated, and everything at its weight in gold; greedy servants who are complaisant only in proportion to your equipage; grovelling towards a rich travelar and insolent towards him whom they suspect of mediocrity".

(Brissot was guillotined in 1793 in the Reign of Terror following the Revolution, but it was for political reasons, not for writing about French inns.)

At Rye, New York, he stopped at "one of the best taverns I have seen in America. It is kept by Mrs. Haviland. We had an excellent dinner and cheap. Two other circumstances very agreeable, which gave us good cheer at this house, the air of the mistress was infinitely graceful and obliging; and she has a charming daughter, genteel and well educated, who played very well the forte-piano."

One can only assume that this is not the same French hotel that had so dismayed Mme Knight when she stayed at Rye ninety years earlier. Nevertheless for all the comfort in the inns, travel itself was rugged.

The journey to New York from Boston (a little over two hundred miles) took up to a week. The carriages were old and much of the harness and shackling was made of ropes. One pair of horses carried the stage eighteen miles. If the journey was uneventful the coach arrived at the resting place for the night at about 10 o'clock and would start the following morning at 2.30 or 3 at the latest.

Thomas Twining wrote of a journey he made in 1795 to Baltimore, Washington, from Philadelphia. "The vehicle was a long car with four benches. Three of these in the interior held nine passengers. A tenth passenger was seated by the side of the driver on the front bench. A light roof was supported by eight slender pillars, four on each side. Three large leather curtains suspended to the roof, one at each side, and the third behind were rolled up or lowered at the pleasure of the passengers. There was no place nor space for luggage each person being expected to stow his things as he could under his seat or legs. The entrance was in front over the driver's bench. Of course, the three passengers were obliged to crawl across all the other benches to get to their places. There were no backs to support and relieve us during a long and fatiguing journey over newly and ill-made roads."

Further, the stages often left before the advertised hour, early as that was, so "many a time an indignant passenger, on time but left behind, was sent off after the coach in a chaise with a single swift horse at full gallop".

Improvement in the service depended, as it had done in Europe, on improvements in the road. For example, there is no record of any inns in Illinois before 1800. Travel was almost entirely by water and travellers slept in their boats or with friends. (The first record of anything like an inn was the building by John Kinzie of a mansion in Chicago to which he added a sixty-foot lodging "for voyagers and Indians".)

In the South, in Mexico and the Spanish territories, the Catholic church provided accommodation for the rare wayfarer and there is no history of any innkeeping before the nineteenth century.

New England, however, was now developing rapidly. "Every ten or fifteen miles," Adam Hodgson wrote in *Among Old New English Inns,* "you come either to a little village composed of a few frame houses with an extensive substantial house, whose respectable appearance, rather than any sign, demonstrates it to be a tavern (as the inns are called) or to a single house appropriated to that purpose and standing alone in the woods. At these taverns you are accosted often with an easy civility ... by a landlord who appears perfectly indifferent whether or not you take anything for the good of the house. If, however, you intimate an intention to take some refreshment, a most plentiful repast is, in due time, set before you, consisting of beef-steaks, fowls, turkies, ham, partridges, eggs and if near the coast fish and oysters with a great variety of hot bread, both of wheat flour and Indian-corn, the latter of which is prepared in many ways and is very good. The landlord usually comes in to converse with you and to make one of the party, and as one cannot have a private room, I do not find his company disagreeable. He is, in general, well informed and well behaved, and the independence of manner which has often been remarked upon, I rather like than otherwise, when it is not assumed or obstrusive but appears to rise naturally from easy circumstances and a consciousness that, both with respect to situation and intelligence, he is at least on a level with the generality of his visitors.

"At first I was a little surprised, on enquiring where the stage stopped to breakfast to be told, at Mayor Todd's—to dine? at Col. Brown's, but I'm now becoming familiar with these phenoma of civil and political equality ..." This independent attitude of American innkeepers fascinated all European visitors who comment on it repeatedly. J. Fenimore Cooper writing about 1840: "The inn-keeper of Old England and the inn-keeper of New England form the very extremes of their class. The one is obsequious to the rich and the other unmoved and often apparently cold. The first seems to calculate at a glance the amount of profit you are likely to leave behind you; while his opposite appears only to calculate in what manner he can most contribute to your comfort without materially impairing his own ... He is often a magistrate, the chief of a battalion of militia, or even a member of a state legislature. He is almost always a man of character; for it is difficult for any other to obtain a licence to exercise the calling."

Unfortunately, Mine Host tended too often to be far more

characterful than hospitable and there are even records of visitors being put in the stocks.

The Rev. Samuel Peters (who had been the pastor of Hartford until chased out by patriots for his pro-British attitude) wrote: "Europeans whose manners were haughty to inferiors and fawning to superiors were neither loved nor esteemed. An English traveller through Connecticut meets with supercilious treatment at taverns, as being too much addicted to the superlative [sic] mood, when speaking to the landlord. 'The answer is command your own servants, not mine.' The traveller is not obeyed which provokes him to some expressions which are not legal in the colony, about the impertinence of the landlord who, being commonly a Justice of the Peace, the delinquent is immediately ordered into custody, fined and put in the stocks. However, after paying the costs and promising to behave well in the future he passes on with more attention to his 'unruly member' than to his pleasures."

The pastor goes on to say how nicely the visitor will be treated if he softens his tone, but this is not the point. Never before in the history of innkeeping does there seem to have been any situation where a dissatisfied guest might find himself behind bars or in the stocks at the discretion of his host. No doubt an actual conviction was a rare event but nowhere else in the world does there ever seem to be a record of a system where disgruntled guests were gruntled in this summary fashion.

When Nathaniel Rogers took over the Marlboro' Hotel in Boston in 1827 (the first American Temperance Hotel) he posted up the following rules.

"Family worship to be attended morning and evening.

"No intoxicating liquors to be sold or used about the house.

"Smoking of cigars not allowed on any part of the premises.

"No money to be received at the office on the Sabbath, nor will any company be received on that day, except in case of necessity.

"Cold and warm baths are provided here for boarders and vegetarian diet for those who prefer it.

"The best efforts are promised by the landlord to furnish the table with the products of free labour."

It will be seen that this makes no mention of swearing—presumably in a temperance hotel such a thing was unthinkable. In the ordinary inn, however, a system of fines for swearing usually applied and accompaniment of the landlord and his family to church services was obligatory as was attendance at family prayers.

Meal times generally were usually the old Puritan ones—breakfast at six, dinner at twelve and supper at six or seven. Guests waited outside the dining room for the door to open and if they were not on time they got nothing.

Apart from their anxiety for the religious welfare of their guests in the New England area there is no doubt that landlords generally regarded themselves as true upholders of democracy and very likely they were.

Colonel Charles Williams hunted, traded and trapped in the Muskingum valley until about 1800 when he built a log tavern and decided to settle down.

Louis Philippe, then the Duke of Orleans, was spending his three years of exile in America at that time and as he travelled up the Muskingum valley he called at Col. Williams' tavern which he found unsatisfactory. When he complained Mine Host replied profanely and to the point. Heat developed with the duke stressing that he was heir to the throne of France and that he was not going to bandy words with a "backwoods plebeian". The colonel retorted that he was an American citizen and every American citizen was a king (this was, in fact, not a figure of speech but a provision of the national and every state constitution).

As kings there may have been some difference in status but as men of action the old Indian scout had it all his own way and he slung the future French king into the road.

Local inhabitants were delighted by this tangible demonstration of what the Republic stood for and until he died (on 2nd August, 1840) the good colonel was elected at one time or another to practically every municipal and county office available and was always thereafter known as "King Charlie".

The independent attitude of the average landlord dated back to the original colonial inns where he sat down with his family and any guests joined them at table to take "pot luck". Mine Host sat at the head, carving, whilst his wife toiled in the kitchen and the youngsters hurried between.

As time passed the "take it or leave it" family meal came to be replaced by meals specially prepared for visitors and nowhere in the world was there a more plentiful supply of food. Venison cost three and a half cents a pound and bear steaks a little more. Anybody with a stick could kill wild pigeons at night as they roosted and it was hard to sell them at a cent each. Wild turkeys weighing from twenty to thirty pounds sold for sixty-two cents and for twelve and a half cents you could buy a sturgeon. Oysters, lobsters and crabs were equally plentiful and cheap.

Even at these prices landlords did not expect to make a profit on their meals—the bar turnover kept them going for while food was cheap and plentiful good cooks were not.

An easy way of getting a reputation for good food in the cow towns and mining camps of the West soon became popular. A menu card from some high-class Eastern restaurant such as Delmonico's would be simply copied in its entirety and stuck up outside some "resteraw" where the sole cooking utensil was a pan. In *The Virginian*, Owen Wister tells of a visitor to a Texan eating house who saw "vol-au-vent" on such a menu and ordered it. The proprietor fingered his six-shooter thoughtfully "Stranger, you'll take hash," he murmured. He took hash.

Naturally, in the boom towns as the West opened, the tavern keeper was likely to have a very easy time without any competition. S. E. White, in his novel *Gold* tells of a group of would-be miners objecting to the prices asked at the *Parker House* in San Francisco.

"I know how you boys feel," the proprietor said. "There's lots in your fix. You'd better stick here tonight and then get organized to camp out, if you're going to be here long. I suppose though, you are going to the mines?"

"There's plenty of gold?" ventured Johnny.

"Bushels."

"I should think you'd be up there."

"I don't want any better gold mine than the old Parker House" he said comfortably.

As the *Parker House* had cost $30,000 to build and, according to Bailey Millard produced a profit of $15,000 a month, one can see his point.

Few hotel proprietors have ever had a chance to coin money as it was coined during San Francisco's gold-rush days. When the boom started thousands of sailors jumped their ships in San Francisco Bay and headed for the diggings. So great was the need for hotels that several of these deserted ships were dragged ashore, held up by posts and became hotels. Later, jerry-built bunk-houses were run up with bunks in three tiers on either side of a narrow passage. Charges for these bunks varied from $30 a week down to $6. In the latter the sleepers lay on straw ticks covered by a single blanket. If there was no blanket left for a latecomer Mine Host took one from a guest already asleep.

Such conditions did not last long, of course—within ten years of gold being found San Francisco had a population of 100,000 and was becoming a real city. Fine hotels like the Palace and the Cosmopolitan were built at a cost of millions of dollars to offer a standard of luxury unexcelled anywhere.

These did not attract the gold miner who sought out the *What Cheer* where he got at $2 a week a clean room complete with an effective delousing service. The restaurant served 4,000 meals a day at an average cost of twenty cents apiece and, as might be expected, the profit was made in the bar. When a miner came into San Francisco he usually went straight to the *What Cheer* and bought a supply of lodging tickets at a cost of fifty cents per night. If he left before using all of these up the *What Cheer* would give him a full refund.

Before the development of better quality accommodation it was naturally still necessary to look back to the East. Here hotels were developing based, as in Europe, around the spas.

In 1722 Yellow Springs and Bath Springs were both discovered and soon there were between 100 and 500 visitors daily during the summer. Various other springs with curative properties were discovered and by 1766 Hot Springs, Virginia, had accommodation for visitors.

The first real resort, however, appears to have been at Bath Springs, Bristol. In 1810 Dr. J. P. Minnick erected a hotel and bathhouse there and in June the following year a Philadelphia paper devoted its leading article to describing it.

"The public spirited proprietor of the hotel and baths of this vicinity," it said, "has been alike liberal of his time and his property to effectuate every purpose of public accommodation. The mansion for the reception of travellers, the offices for the accommodation of domestics, the larder for the luxury of the Gourmand, and the cellar for Bacchus's hoard, all testify that anxious wish to please, which the liberal men of the world cannot fail to appreciate generously."

The public-spirited proprietor had the pleasure of seeing his hotel develop very successfully (it was a great social centre through the Civil War) until Saratoga Springs started to attract attention. Saratoga's first spring was discovered in 1767 but it was not until 1795 that the first building—a log tavern—was erected for visitors. More springs, including Congress Spring, were discovered as the years went by, but there was no real development until 1826 when Dr. Clarke, a Yorkshireman (who had introduced the first soda fountain to New York) bought the farm on which Congress Spring stood. There were twenty other springs near and the enterprising doctor had them tapped and started to bottle and sell the water. Soon afterwards he built a hotel, the Congress Hall, a very elegant building with spacious piazzas, gardens and pine groves accommodating 200 guests.

Other hotels were being built and Saratoga Springs began to attract wealthy and fashionable sufferers. About now seaside resorts were beginning to attract visitors for the first time. Hotel keepers at Long Branch endeavoured to have the best of both worlds by buying barrels of Congress Spring water to sell at the seaside. Dr. Clarke would have none of this so Long Branch simply named a near-by stream the Saratoga Spring and supplied their own home-brewed Saratoga water without difficulty.

What they could not supply so easily and what Saratoga soon became famous for, was a steady supply of brides and eligible young men. For all the talk of sulphur springs and cures it soon became clear that in the season these famous watering places were basically a marriage market. (The early European spas had had lower aspirations.) American hotels advertized their "Lover's Walk" or "Courtship Maze" and Saratoga had a "Courting Yard with proposal sofas" in various sequestered nooks ("I say, after you with the sofa old chap, do you think you'll be long?" or "I'm sure he meant to, mama, but there was no sofa free").

Some such attraction was necessary to provide an interest, for in the early days there was little recreation.

As E. A. Kendall recounts rather gloomily in his *Travel through the Northern Parts of the United States*:

"The evenings at the Springs were generally spent by the young women in singing hymns of which a favourite one was called the Garden Hymn, beginning 'The Lord is to his Garden come,' etc. They sing hymns because they are more familiar with the words and tunes of these than with those of songs and because they are accustomed to sing them in parts. A clergyman happening to come among us, prayers, hymns and chapters of the Bible were quoted before breakfast."

It was in Saratoga that the first temperance society was formed in 1808 but other forces were at work there and on 4th July, 1848, Patten and Cole opened a racecourse with prizes from fifty to two hundred dollars and "other purses as liberal as the proprietors can afford".

Soon racing and gambling became Saratoga's main attractions and gradually the better class visitor looked elsewhere.

White Sulphur Springs was even more famous for its matchmaking as the blushing beauties of the entire South sought to visit it and Harrison Rhodes tells of purses being made up in little Southern towns to send likely maidens to the "Old White" as late as 1880. J. H. B. Latrobe was an architect who visited White Sulphur in 1832 and found it "a pleasant place to live. There is something eminently aristocratic about the place and you feel

that you are with your fellows here . . ." Just how aristocratic is
not quite clear for he goes on:

"In the hands of the Yankees it might become a veritable
paradise . . . a little management would soon introduce order
where all now is confusion.

"Crowds collect around the dining room and when the doors
are opened there is a rush, like that at the booth at a contest elec-
tion. Every man, woman and child rush to any seat which they
may happen to find and in a very short time the food upon the
tables disappears, consumed by the hungry mob. If you have a
servant of your own, he must bribe the cook. If you have no
servant, you must bribe one of those attached to the place, or
you run the risk of getting nothing. Bribery furnishes you with
the best of what is to be got in the place, and avoids the rushes
at meal time. The day after I arrived two waiters quarrelled over
an apple pie; one floored the other and neither got the pie which
was floored in the scuffle—and this scene took place while the
guests were seated at table. Bribe high and you live high; fail to
bribe and you starve; look sharp and eat fast, you forget good
manners. This is the motto of the dining room of the White
Sulphur."

Meantime, in New York the first skyscraper was being built.
This was the *Adelphi Hotel* erected in 1827 and a full six storeys
high. This was long before the day of the steel frame building
(and also of the elevator!) so this was about the maximum safe
height.

The last big inn to be built in New York was *Holt's*. Stephen
B. Holt ran a "one shilling plate and two shilling ordinary" at
the Fulton Market and dreamed of his own hotel. For six years
his wife, Mary, worked with her needle; this was before the days
of the sewing machine. She stitched 1,500 towels, 400 pairs of
sheets, 400 pairs of pillow-cases "all ruffled and pointed", 250
bed ticks and 300 patchwork bed quilts, some made of pieces no
bigger than a penny. Meantime, her husband was getting his
hotel built. He knew there was no chance of going higher than
the Adelphi, but he was not to be excelled and his hotel was also
a six-storey one.

Unfortunately, the site he had chosen was too far from the fashionable Broadway. It smacked of the sea and it was patronized mainly by skippers and pursers and ship's doctors. On the roof was a walk, railed in by ornamental iron-works—the "captain's walk". It has been suggested that this was New York's first roof garden.

Holt's was the first hotel to have a steam-power hoisting apparatus to lift luggage, but not passengers, to upper floors. It had 225 rooms and the *Journal of Commerce* called it the "wonder of New York". Charges were about $1.50 a day and $10 to $12 a week.

As an inn it was perhaps impressive. But the first true hotel had already been built and Holt never had a chance.

CHAPTER 8

THE FIRST HOTEL

In some countries, like Spain, there actually has appeared an impression that the word "Hilton" is English for "Hotel".

Life International 21/10/63

THE first hotel that was ever invented, the *Tremont*, opened in Boston, Massachusetts, on 16th October, 1829. Inn-keeping had developed naturally over the years in the same way that we came to walk upright or eat cooked food. It was an American claim that there is as big a difference between the old inn and the modern hotel as between a broom and a vacuum cleaner; that the modern luxury hotel is as much an invention as the sewing machine and that it was an American invention, the first transatlantic development that owed nothing to Europe.

The word hotel came from France—hotel was a later form of hostel which came from the Latin hospitale. Just as the word *inn* had originally meant a large house in England, so in France *hotel* meant a large private residence or town mansion. There had been a tendency for large inns to be built on the lines of these big town houses. Indeed in Italy in the fifteenth century inns or hotels were being built very similar to the palaces. There was one in Padua in 1450 with stabling for 200 horses and, literally, palatial accommodation for guests.

However, these few elaborate European hotels were for an exclusive minority, and did not function as we think of hotels today. Usually the guest took a room or a suite of rooms and his own servant or retinue accompanied him to prepare meals and provide service generally. We get some indication of what the better-class traveller might expect by considering the arrangements on ships making long voyages—to India for instance. Right up to the last century the passenger was provided with an empty cabin for which he had to supply all his own furniture, to be sold at a heavy loss at the end of the voyage.

There is little doubt that the opening of the *Tremont* was the start of what we now know as the American Way of Life.

The world's first hotel architect was Isaiah Rogers. He had the field to himself and although there were plenty who were critical of the result, few architects ever manage to please so many of the public as Rogers did.

The building was large, probably the largest and certainly the costliest in the country at that time. Three storeys high, it took an entire block on Tremont Street and had 170 rooms, a dozen public rooms (unknown then) and the main dining room could seat no less than 200 diners.

The general line was simple, based on Greek classicism. The style was to be copied by most other hotel architects and for half a century Rogers' idea of how a hotel should look dominated the world.

The ceilings were high, floors of black and white marble squares (or else completely carpeted) and the furniture native carved walnut. Good curtaining and first-class French decorating completed the picture. Americans, and particularly Bostonians, were ecstatic. Even possible critics like Thomas Hamilton of Blackwood's staff were so pleased with the standard of catering and service that they stifled other thoughts and did not feel "to be compelled to speak disparagingly of its architecture".

For the *Tremont* was new and different in every way. Outside it had no inn sign. Inn signs were legally required in New England to assist illiterate travellers. The *Tremont* was not looking for illiterate travellers.

At the opening banquet the bill of fare was a printed facsimile of handwriting, the first time this had been done in America and banker guests looked worriedly at the printed signature of the proprietor, Dwight Boyden, across the bottom.

There appears no evidence of menus being printed before the

Tremont was opened for when guests had all dined communally all the food had been put on the table and a bill of fare served no purpose. It had been common in old-time inns for mine host to call out descriptions of food as he carved "Here's a rare slice for Mrs. A.—Ah, a nice bone cut for Col. B. Pass your plate, Miss J., for this splendid cut."

General McMackin had a hotel in Vicksburg, Mississippi, and he called out from the carving table "Nice turkey hash, fresh sausages, cold ham, the best beefsteak in the world" while he carved and directed the waiters. Bishop Pierce wrote of him, "All his various directions worked into a sort of song; and were it not that the tune is a nondescript one might imagine that the old Roman fashion of combining music and feasting had been revived on the banks of the Mississippi. This plan is a substitute for printed bills of fare, now common in all the best city hotels. He says, I understand, that the reason he adopted this unique method was that some years ago he kept a public house in Jackson and many of his boarders were members of the legislature and could not read, so he had to call out for their information. Finding it cheap and easy he had continued it."

Normally, inn guests had washed in the bar or the kitchen or even out in the yard. At the better establishments a service was beginning of providing a bowl of water in the bedroom but the *Tremont* did this without being asked and, further, provided a piece of soap free. It was only a hard yellow lump, far from the scented cakes of today, but then soap was a costly item and the *Tremont's* liberality was unheard of.

It was typical of the new standard in commercial hospitality set by the *Tremont*. It became so much an accepted feature of hotel life in America and Great Britain too—that when, half a century later, Mark Twain found that such a practice was not normal throughout the world, or even throughout Europe, he was astounded.

"At every hotel we stop at we always have to send out for soap, at the last moment, when we are grooming ourselves for dinner, and they put it on the bill with the candles and other nonsense. In Marseilles they make half the fancy toilet soap we consume in

America, but the Marseillaise only have a vague theoretical idea of its use, which they have obtained from books of travel just as they have acquired an uncertain notion of clean shirts and the peculiarities of the gorilla, and other curious matters. This reminds me of poor Blucher's note to the landlord in Paris.

" 'M. le Landlord. Sir. Pourquoi don't you mettez some savon in your bedchambers? Est ce que vous pensez I will steal it? La nuit passe you charge me pour deux chandelles when I only had one: hier vous avez charged me avec glace when I had none at all; tout les jours you are coming some fresh game or other on me, mais vous ne pouvez pas play this savon dodge on me twice. Savon is a necessary de la vie to anybody but a Frenchman et je l'aurai hors de cet hotel or make trouble. You hear me. Alons. Blucher.'

"Blucher said he guessed the old man could read the French of it and average the rest."

It was the *Tremont* that put a tablet of soap into hotel bedrooms around the world, although you still cannot be sure of it in many countries today.

No doubt water would have been piped up to the bedrooms had it been possible, but plumbing then could not yet raise water above the ground floor level. Most of the *Tremont's* facilities were in the basement and were well worth the walk down (there were no passenger lifts yet). Not only were there eight "bathing rooms" next to the laundry, but there was also a block of eight water closets. There may have been an odd water closet here and there in the mansions of the wealthier citizens but, generally, this was a luxury almost unheard of and apparently unknown in a public building in America at that time.

The Reading Room would appear strange to us today. There were no public libraries then and very few on a private subscription basis. The *Tremont* provided a room stocked with newspapers from all over the States and from Europe. Guests had free access and the public could enter on payment of a small fee. This arrangement became a very popular feature and for the next half century most hotels had some similar reading room.

A startling innovation was the annunciator. This was the first device ever patented that had been designed solely for use in hotels. Previously, a visitor to an inn could attract attention by ringing a handbell or simply shouting. This sufficed where there were only a few guest rooms, but was hardly satisfactory in large establishments. Seth Fuller designed the electro-magnetic annunciator which enabled the guest to press a button in his room and in the office a buzzer sounded and a metal disc dropped to show which room required service.

Or such was the theory. "One ring for ice-water, two for bellboy, three for porter, four for chambermaid and not a darned one of them will come," one critic commented sourly, but he was not speaking of the *Tremont*.

The annunciator was invaluable before the days of room telephone, and indeed, the Paris Ritz today still uses push buttons for floor service.* When Holland House (no connection with Lady Holland) opened in New York in 1889 each room had an annunciator with a dial listing one hundred and forty different articles. The guest turned the dial to the article he wanted, pressed the button and the staff did the rest.

The annunciator was part of another feature of the new *Tremont*: the introduction of room service. It had always been taken for granted that visitors ate in a hotel at the time that the proprietor fixed. Thomas Hamilton considered the American hotel manager as "the most rigorous and iron-hearted of despots ... and surely never was a monarch blessed with more patient and obedient subjects. He feeds them in droves like cattle. He rings a bell and they come like dogs at their master's whistle. He

---

* On each bedside table are four buttons, marked chambermaid, valet, waiter and Service Privé. The last is for those of us who travel with our own servants. These are given rooms in which our Service Privé bell rings.
In fact, nowadays there is little demand for this particular accommodation, but until the beginning of this century any hotel or any host had to be prepared to cater for his guests' private servants. When Lady Holland visited Woburn in 1815, for instance, she had a retinue of no less than sixteen. The Duke felt this a bit much, with such problems as that of the chamber pot. Instead of relying on the ducal porcelain she had brought her own solid silver article. At Woburn maids cleaned the china and under-butlers looked after the plate. Lady Holland was thus, rather thoughtlessly, responsible for one of the first labour demarcation disputes.

places before them what he thinks proper and they swallow it without grumbling."

He did not complain about the *Tremont*, however, for he "enjoyed the blessing of rational liberty, had command of my own hours and motions: in short, could eat, drink or sleep at what time, in what manner and on what substances I might prefer".

Charles Dickens also indicates the anxiety of the staff to meet his requirements. The point of the amusing little story is lost today when we are so familiar with the phrase "Right away" which at that time was an Americanism quite meaningless to the great novelist.

" 'Dinner if you please,' said I to the waiter.

" 'When?' said the waiter.

" 'As quick as possible,' said I.

" 'Right away?' said the waiter.

"After a moment's hesitation I answered, 'No,' at hazard.

" 'Not right away?' cried the waiter with an amount of surprise that made me start.

"I looked at him doubtfully and returned, 'No, I would rather have it in this private room. I like it very much.'

"At this I really thought the waiter must have gone out of his mind as I believe he would have done, but for the interposition of another man who whispered in his ear, 'Directly'.

" 'Well! and that's a fact,' said the waiter looking helplessly at me. 'Right away.'

"I saw now that 'Right Away' and 'Directly' were one and the same thing. So I reversed my previous answer and sat down to dinner in ten minutes afterwards, and a capital dinner it was.

"The hotel (a very excellent one) is called the *Tremont House*. It has more galleries, colonnades, piazzas and passages than I can remember or the reader would believe."

Another writer who was very impressed by the *Tremont* was Thackeray. He had made some comment in England about American oysters which he had heard were an enormous size. When he visited Boston he stayed at the *Tremont* where his hosts had secured the largest oysters they could find. However, they took care before the meal to apologize "for what we call the extreme smallness of the oysters, promising better next time. Six bloated Falstaffian bivalves lay before him in their shells . . . he selected the smallest one . . . struggled for a moment and then all was over. I shall never forget the comic look of despair he cast upon the other five over-occupied shells. I broke the perfect stillness by asking him how he felt? 'Profoundly grateful,' he gasped —'and as if I had swallowed a little baby'. "

Tyrone Power, the Irish actor, stayed at the *Tremont* in 1883 and was astonished by the quantities of food. At seven-thirty a.m. the crash of the gong aroused all sleepers and at eight breakfast was served. Dinner was at three, tea at six, supper at nine. "It is yet a marvel to me," wrote Power, "first how all these elaborate meals are so admirably got up, and next, how the plague these good people find appetite to come to time with a regularity no less surprising."

To tempt their appetites proprietor Boyden had imported from Europe the classic French cuisine. The *Tremont* was the first American hotel ever to have a French chef.

There were already French restaurants which had originally developed from New Orleans. When the French Revolution of 1789 occurred many of the leading French chefs fled abroad. They had been the pampered darlings of the aristocrats and as the Reign of Terror went on and supplies of aristocracy grew short many chefs thought it wise to depart. New Orleans was the one purely French corner of America and there they naturally gravitated.

In 1794 *Juliens Restarator* was opened in Boston, the first French restaurant in the North. It was a success and about 1800 another refugee, Francis Guerin, opened a restaurant in New York. They had an uphill struggle to conquer American prejudice. The basis of classic French cooking is limitless trouble over the most minute detail with every possible elaboration of sauce and frills. Americans did not like frills. Generally, they felt with Owen Wister's Virginian that "it would give an outraged stomach to a plain-raised man".

Fortunately, there were plenty of visitors to the *Tremont* who did not want to be regarded as plain-raised men and the French cuisine was a complete success. Soon as new hotels were built a demand was created for French chefs who were even attracted from France by the high wages offered—sometimes as much as $125 a month.

By 1852 all first-class hotels had the French cuisine and with only one exception used French terms on their menus. Only the *Astor House* insisted on giving English names to all dishes "capable of translation".

Wealthy families then began to employ French chefs in their own kitchens, and the Astors, Vanderbilts and Goulds vied to give the most elaborate dinners. By 1870 a hotel chef could command a salary of up to $250 a month and in 1877 the *Hotel Mail* poured scorn on the rumour that the chef of the St. George Hotel in Philadelphia was being paid $300 a month. The *Mail* considered this simply absurd but six years later the Hoffman House in New York paid this to tempt the head chef of the Café d'Anglais from Paris.*

John Jacob Astor, the first great American tycoon, watched the success of the *Tremont* with great interest. If a place like Boston could support the *Tremont* then he calculated that New York should have something still better. He set about getting it in a very simple way. The same architect, Isaiah Rogers, was commissioned to design it, and the same family, the Boydens were appointed to run it. The new hotel would thus become a larger, improved version of the *Tremont* incorporating all the afterthoughts and lessons that that hotel had taught. It was to be

---

* Meantime, private employers were paying up to $5,000 a year for their chefs and it was said that George W. Childs paid his chef $8,000 a year. Most famous of all, perhaps, was M. Thouraud. He had been chef to President Faure and the Duc de Rochefoucauld and then succeeded Escoffier at the Savoy. He was tempted over to the U.S. with eight assistants to prepare a single banquet for a railroad king.

W. K. Vanderbilt approached him then and persuaded him to join his household. The great chef was dubious from the start. Very soon he found that his new master's favourite dish was corned beef and cabbage and he was asked continually to prepare this. When this happened four times in one week, it was too much for the virtuoso who carried 2,000 recipes in his head. "You do not need a chef, M'sieur," he announced, "but a gardener." He packed his bags and returned to a world where his timbales de filets de sole and poulet Polonaise received the respect that was their due.

erected on Broadway from Barclay to Vesey Street, where Astor himself had lived until then.

Whilst the *Astor* was being built a few blocks away *Holt's Hotel*—"the wonder of New York"—was failing tragically. It was badly placed and hardly survived two years. Holt went bankrupt and on 1st October, 1835, the six-storey skyscraper and all its contents, including all Mrs. Holt's careful handiwork, was sold for $175,000. Holt lingered on penniless, trying in his old age to retrieve his fortune in the restaurant business that he knew, but he died, unsuccessful, at the age of seventy-one.

Work on the *Astor* was completed in May the next year, 1836. There was a massive granite front on to Broadway and the usual Isaiah Rogers' Doric portal. There were the same public rooms as in the *Tremont* only they were larger (the hotel itself was two storey's higher); there were seventeen bathing rooms and two showers in the basement and the *New Yorker* (4th June, 1836) reported that the rooms "were all fitted up and furnished in a style of unostentatious richness and severe simplicity, the sofas, bureaus, tables and chairs from basement to attic being uniformly of a beautiful black walnut, while the floors are as regularly overlaid with superior oilcloth of various tasteful patterns". There were 309 rooms and Astor seems to have got good value for the $400,000 he spent.

When the hotel was opened the Mayor made a speech commenting that the hotel was virtually a palace which "for centuries to come will serve as a monument, as it is probably intended, to its wealthy proprietor". In fact as a monument it was not a great success and only lasted ten years.

The *New York Constellation* reported "the house is lighted by this gas everybody is discussing; but the quantity consumed being greater than common, it gave out suddenly in the midst of a cotillion. Gas is a handsome light but liable at all times to give the company the slip and it is illy calculated for the ordinary use of the family."

Gas generally was a constant problem to hotel proprietors in its early days because unsophisticated guests kept blowing out the gaslight in their bedrooms, as they might blow out a candle, so that Bill Nye remarked, "the door of our room is full of holes where locks have been wrenched off in order to let the coroner in".

Indeed, Simeon Ford, the landlord of the *Grand Union Hotel* in New York, was plagued by guests who chose his establishment in which to commit suicide.

He never canvassed for this class of trade, he wrote, "and yet when a man feels it is time for him to shuffle off this mortal coil, it seems perfectly natural for him to drift into our hotel, unostentatious though it may be. It is a comparatively easy class of trade to satisfy. They do not stop to enquire whether the plumbing is modern or antique . . . give them a good six-foot gas-burner, about 1,500 feet of illuminating gas at $1 a thousand and a few uninterrupted minutes and they are content." He goes on to write of a bridegroom complaining that he had learned that his honeymoon night had been spent in a room where two people had just committed suicide. "I said, my dear sir, you would hardly expect us to put a silver plate on the door, and silver handles and consecrate the room to the memory of the dear departed. We are conducting a hotel not a cemetery."

Hard, perhaps, but would-be suicides are a particular problem for the hotel-keeper. Ernest Henderson, for instance, tells of an early advertising campaign his Sheraton Hotel Company launched. Small scatter ads—four or five two-inch-square insertions scattered in the "run of the paper would present our message at moderate cost. The programme was launched with breathless anticipation.

"We selected the *New York Times* for this important campaign. Unfortunately a zealous *Times* reporter had despatched on that very day a story from Detroit which appeared on an inside page. The heading read 'Prominent New Yorker jumps from 14th floor of Detroit's Sheraton Hotel'. The articles described the victim's distinguished career, a list of his many achievements and told of the widow left behind. His clubs were duly enumerated, but there still was space at the bottom of the column—just enough for one of our small ads. It carried our slogan current at the time 'Always try Sheraton first'."

The scale and the success of the great luxury hotels fascinated European visitors. "Everything appears large," wrote the Rev. George Lewis, "a large ante-room for smoking and lounging and reading the newspapers—spacious parlours and a still more spacious hall where the common meals of breakfast, dinner and supper (our tea) are served. Travellers come in twenties and fifties to our dozens. You live in a crowd—eat in a crowd, sitting down with fifty, a hundred, sometimes two hundred at a table to which you are summoned by a sonorous Chinese gong. The only place of retirement is your room, to which you have a key."

This typical American crowd living was not always to the taste of European visitors, for example, when Anthony Trollope's mother, Mrs. Frances Trollope, visited Cincinnati and stayed at the *Washington Tavern*, she asked the waitress to serve her tea in her rooms. Shortly afterwards, the landlord appeared. "Any person ill?" he enquired gruffly. Everybody was well. "Then, madam, I must tell you I cannot accommodate you on these terms; we have no family tea-drinking here and you must either eat with my wife, or me, or not at all in my house." She explained that she had not known the manners of the country— hence her mistake. "Our manners are very good manners and we don't wish any changes from England," he retorted. One wonders at the level of conversation at the subsequent enforced communal meals . . . However, the landlord was not merely being difficult, as Mrs. Trollope, assumed. It was not part of the American way of life to encourage guests to be aloof.

When Monnot opened the aristocratic *New York Hotel* he not only offered meals à la carte and cooked to order, but announced that his hotel would specialize in private dining (or room service).

This was fifteen years after the *Tremont* in Boston had discreetly started to provide the same facilities but New Yorkers were shocked by the public announcement of this reversal of accepted practice.

"There are some republican advantages in our present system of hotels which the country is not yet ready to forego," snarled N. P. Willis in the *New York Weekly Mirror* (7th December, 1844). "Tell a country lady in these times that when she comes to New York she must eat and pass the evening in a room by herself and she would rather stay at home. The going to the *Astor* and dining with two hundred well-dressed people and sitting in full dress in a splendid drawing room with plenty of company is the charm of going to the city. The theatres are nothing to that. Broadway, the shopping and the sights, are all subordinate—poor accessories to the main object of the visit." He went on to make the point that life in hotel public rooms was "the tangible republic —the only thing palpable and agreeable that we have to show, in common life, as republican . . . and when the hotel-garni draws its dividing line through this promiscuous community of habits the cords will be cut which will let some people Up, out of reach, and drop some people Down, out of all satisfactory supportable contact with society."

However, no great harm appeared to come to the republic and soon great hotels were being built across the country—New Orleans, Philadelphia, Washington, Baltimore; in rapid succession they opened their *St. Louis, Lafayette, Gilmore, Girard* or *Continental* hotels. The *American Hotel* in Buffalo was held to be every bit as good as the *Astor*. It burned down in 1850, was rebuilt and burned again in 1865.

Every opening was proclaimed with lavish publicity. Descriptions of the furnishings were always accompanied by details of the cost—the *Irving House* cost half a million to build and a hundred and fifty thousand dollars more for furniture. The first hotel to break through the million dollar barrier was the *St. Nicholas* in New York—six storeys of white marble.

Gold embroidered draperies cost a thousand dollars and window curtains seven hundred dollars each. Huge chandeliers blazed light through a riot of coloured prisms, there were mirrors everywhere and any surface at all that could take gold leaf was gilded. A visiting English comedian said he would be afraid to put his shoes outside the door to be shined for fear the management would gild them.

One of the great features of the *St. Nicholas Hotel* were the beds. They had sprung mattresses. The ordinary bed had a base of slats or cords on which lay a hair or flock mattress. This had been accepted for centuries and then in 1831 a Mr. J. French from Massachusetts invented the bed spring. They had to be hand made and so sprung mattresses were rare and costly. It was not until 1871 that a machine was invented to produce bed springs.

The *St. Nicholas* may not have been the very first hotel to install spring beds (there is no record) but they were sufficiently a novelty to impress the *Tribune*: "The beds consist of a sommier elastique or spring mattress with a heavy hair mattress upon it —better could not be" (3rd December, 1852).

Even more attractive than the spring beds were some of the rooms in which they stood—the bridal chambers. This was a coy feature that had first been introduced when the *Irving Hotel* opened five years before. These "fairy boudoirs" inspired the *Tribune*, which thought of them as love bowers "where Eve might have whispered love to Adam after she was expelled from Paradise without regretting the change".

The *Tribune* had got over its delighted shock by the time the *St. Nicholas Hotel* opened and was able to give more details. The rooms were "lined and ornamented throughout with the purest of white satin—with an exquisite canopy of white satin gathered in heavy folds at each corner, falling over a bed of lace and white satin, which is also surrounded by cushions of white satin". More chandeliers, gold leaf and a massive carved four-poster bed. "Its bridal chambers are scandalously splendid," commented *Putnam's Magazine*, "and timid brides are said to shrink aghast at its marvels of white satin and silver brocade". Well they might have done but bridal chambers were good business just the same.

Building with steel framework and then the passenger lift enabled architects to break through the six-storey barrier at last. The first passenger elevator was installed in the *Fifth Avenue Hotel* in New York. This was a hotel used by Republicans whilst the Democrats gathered in the *Hoffman House*. It was Mark Twain who commented that an honest man in politics shines more than he would elsewhere and it seems likely that in one of these hotels (who would suggest which?) the definition of a "straight politician" was first heard. A "straight politician", you will recall, was one who, when squared, stayed squared.

More and better hotels continued to appear: there was nothing anywhere else in the world like this. G. A. Sala had to explain to his English readers: "The American hotel is to an English hotel what an elephant is to a periwinkle, to borrow a simile from Tupper's Ode to Chaos. . . . An American hotel is (in the chief cities) as roomy as Buckingham Palace and is not much inferior to a palace in its internal fittings. It has ranges of drawing rooms, suites of private rooms, vast staircases and interminable layers of bedchambers."

In fact, the *National Intelligencia* had already described these hotels as "the palaces of the people" and there is little doubt that they did typify much of the great American dream.

The wife of an immigrant from the ghettoes and slums of Europe striving grimly to establish a home in a queer foreign land could dream of the day when her daughter would marry and honeymoon in such luxury. There were none of the class barriers of Europe—so long as a visitor had the dollars there was nothing to stop him going into these great luxury hotels.

So they came to be built across the country, often sited rather unwisely and built more as a gesture of faith than a commercial proposition. The leading citizens who believed in their town wanted to see it have a suitable hotel, worthy of its future. In many cases building the town's hotel seemed to have much in common with the spirit that drove medieval Europeans to create their great churches and cathedrals.

The *St. Charles Hotel* in New Orleans, for example, was claimed at the time to be the finest in the world and yet was a financial disaster to its original proprietors. Opened on 22nd February, 1837, it cost $800,000 and had a great gilded dome in imitation of the National Capitol.

The Creoles scorned this hotel built with Yankee money and proceeded to build their own *St. Louis Hotel*. This was to be immortalized in *Uncle Tom's Cabin*, as one of the great slave auction centres of the South.

After early difficulties both the *St. Charles* and the *St. Louis* settled down to long periods of prosperity interrupted by the usual disastrous fires. The *St. Louis* burned down in 1841 and was rebuilt and the *St. Charles* in 1850 and, again in 1894 by which time even the Creoles were beginning to boast of it.

The smaller *St. Louis* was their particular pride, however, and in 1845 the Louisiana legislature adjourned from Jackson (as being too inconvenient) and held its sessions in the ballroom of the *St. Louis*. In 1874 the State bought out the hotel and used it as a State House. After ten years it reverted to a hotel—the *Hotel Royal*—but now the magic was gone—as had so much else in the South by then. Eventually, the *St. Louis* closed and was finally demolished in 1914 but, perhaps symbolically, the Yankee *St. Charles* continued to flourish.

In 1830 the town of St. Louis was a little fur post with a population of less than 5,000 and a tavern called the *Planter's Hotel*. Then the town started to grow on the Mississippi River traffic and in 1841 the second *Planter's Hotel* was built by a community stock company at a cost of $100,000. The town, by now with a population of 20,000, could boast that they had a hotel comparable with any in the East and with a ballroom "larger than that of the celebrated *Tremont House* in Boston". Fortunately, St. Louis continued to grow so its ambitious hotel flourished and eventually had to be rebuilt in 1894.

A more startling example of faith in a town's future was "Couch's Folly". On 8th December, 1828, the Commissioners of Peoria County issued a licence to Archibald Caldwell who thus became the first tavern keeper in Chicago. It was only a little log tavern and after a year Caldwell decided that there was more future in the busy fur-trading post of Green Bay, Wisconsin, than there ever would be in a little backwoods village like Chicago.

Elijah Wentworth was heading West from Maine with his wife and four children when he reached the banks of the Wabash in October 1829. Bad weather stopped them for a while and when he heard that Caldwell was leaving his tavern Wentworth decided to take over the lease. It was a good decision, the trickle of visitors from the East was increasing steadily and soon the little town could support no less than three taverns and then, in 1835, a brick hotel.

That same year a hotel called *Tremont House* was also built, which burned down in 1839 and its successor opened the next year and burned down in 1849. Two brothers, Ira and James Couch, had been in the hotel business for thirteen years and they thought that Chicago, which now had a population of 28,000 would grow still more. They did not, therefore, merely rebuild the third *Tremont House*, they bought additional land and covered the entire site with a huge building five and a half storeys high. It only cost $75,000 but in 1850 $75,000 bought a lot of hotel and the Couches had a veritable palace. "There is perhaps no hotel in the Union superior to it in any respect," pontificated the editor of the *Gem of the Prairies* rather optimistically. "Its internal arrangements, including furniture and decorations, are all in the highest style of art, and of the class denominated princely."

Nevertheless, it was so very much too big for the foreseeable future that Chicagoans fondly termed it Couch's Folly and agreed entirely when they read that it was "wholly uncalled for by the demand of the times".

Within two years, however, two more railway lines, the Michigan Southern and the Michigan Central reached Chicago from the East and it was possible to travel from New York (if all went well) in forty-eight hours. Within ten years the population of Chicago had bounded up fourfold and by 1868 Couch's Folly had been enlarged twice and had 300 rooms, not to mention "Atwood's celebrated improved passenger elevator" and its ten thousand dollar "Ladies Parlor".

Other hotels had, of course, been rushed up and in 1869 a guide book listed no less than twenty first-class hotels as well as numerous inferior ones.

In 1870 Potter Palmer built what he claimed to be the "only fireproof hotel in the world"—the *Palmer House*—and exactly fifty-three weeks later—on 8th October, 1871, it was one of the first to be burned down in the great Chicago fire. The new *Grand Pacific Hotel* had not been open a week but it blazed the same way as did Couch's Folly and all the rest of the biggest and best hotels in the city.

A similar fate befell the *Palace Hotel* in San Francisco. This hotel had been built by W. C. Ralston, head of the Bank of California, to accommodate twelve hundred people, with an initial cost of over four million dollars. This was more than ten times what Astor had paid for his hotel in New York and was intended to show the sort of place San Francisco really was. Unfortunately, Ralston ran into difficulties before the work was complete and drowned himself.

A colleague, Senator William Sharon, completed the hotel as his friend had intended and it was opened in 1875. It was vast. There were 755 rooms, each twenty feet square, laid out in the shape of a hollow quadrangle with a crystal roof over the interior court. This had a tropical garden with statues and fountains and band concerts were given morning and afternoon. Naturally, every effort was made to construct the *Palace* to be fireproof. The foundation walls were twelve feet thick and on these arose the seven-storey structure in a 3,000-ton wrought iron skeleton. From basement to roof the iron staircases were in brick and stone compartments to avoid the "chimney" effect in a fire. On the roof were seven tanks holding 130,000 gallons of water with five times that much under the centre court, in reserve, backed by four artesian wells and three large fire pumps. There were 15,000 feet of special fire hose distributed over the floors, self-acting fire alarms and a half hourly fire patrol.

The *Palace Hotel* burned down in the great fire following the 1906 earthquake. The architects had planned for everything except crass stupidity. The hotel withstood the earthquake shock and there was no fire damage except from surrounding property. This could be handled by the judicious use of the water stored for this very purpose. What nobody had foreseen was that as the fire advanced municipal offices were threatened. Martial law was declared and under it, the city fathers took the *Palace*'s water in an effort to save their offices. In the end the offices and the hotel were all destroyed.

It had not actually been the biggest hotel in the world because two months before it opened the *United States Hotel* had been opened in Saratoga and that had nearly a thousand rooms. Anybody in San Francisco, however, could have explained to you that that was merely a summer hotel whilst the *Palace* was the largest city hotel.

In fact, it would perhaps not be untrue to say that there were few towns in America which could not at one time or another truthfully boast—even if only for a few weeks—that it had the biggest, or the costliest, or the highest, or the finest hotel in the world.

There had never been anything like this in history and E. L. Godkin wrote in the *Nation* (11th September, 1884) that American hotels were "the wonder of the Old World and formed a prominent feature in the tales of all travellers who had crossed the Atlantic. Their size, the perfection of their organization, the lavishness and excellence of their table were constant subjects of admiration in European newspapers. In fact, they were so much talked about that at least the belief was spread in England, and is firmly held in England by large numbers of people to this day, that all Americans lived in hotels and that home life in a house was almost unknown on this side of the Atlantic. There was nothing in England, or in France or Switzerland either, except a very few expensive hotels, at which great personages on their travels took 'suites of apartments' which no man of moderate means dared to enter." No such problem existed in God's Own Country for the man of moderate means. Every citizen was a king and the hotel was his palace so long as he had the price in his pocket.

CHAPTER 9

THE HOTEL DE LUXE

There is only one difference between a waiter and the devil; a
waiter has two tails.

J. M. Eggle, Head of the Cellars, the Savoy

M. ESCHER, the proprietor of the *Hotel des Trois Couronnes et
Poste* in 1865 was a kindly man, loath to dismiss any staff. More-
over, the lad of fifteen years before him was the son of an old
friend. Still the truth had to be faced and it would be unfair to
encourage him to pursue the wrong career.

"You will never make anything of yourself in the hotel business," he said at last; "it requires a special flair and I must tell
you the truth—you don't have it."

So César Ritz lost his first job, as an apprentice wine waiter.
His father, the owner of a smallholding in the Swiss village of
Niederwald, had paid 300 francs to have him taught the trade
in neighbouring Brig. Ashamed to return home, he found another job as an assistant waiter. He was soon dismissed and
drifted to Paris where the Universal Exhibition was to be held
and so he expected that there would be a demand for temporary
staff in hotels. There was, but it did not help him much. Eventually, he was working as a waiter in a cheap workmen's bistro and
he lost this job too, for breaking too many plates.

It was hardly an auspicious start to a great career. Nobody
could have forseen that he was to make his name, easily read or
pronounced in any language, a world-wide synonym for luxury.
Ritz was seventeen before, for some reason, he became ambitious.
Perhaps it was a love affair, his first, with "une charmante baronne

russe". Perhaps he merely realized that there was no great difficulty in starving to death in nineteenth-century Europe.

At any rate he worked hard in his next job in another small restaurant and soon was appointed restaurant manager. He then conceived the idea of becoming a waiter at *Voisin*, the most fashionable house in Paris, where statesmen and generals watched the arrival of Sarah Bernhardt or George Sand or the departure of the younger Dumas. His employer tried to hold him with the offer of a partnership, but Ritz went to Bellenger, the proprietor of *Voisin* and begged for a job where "I could start at the beginning and learn, if you will teach me".

This appealed to Bellenger who gave him a chance. He did well again and soon great and famous men began to ask for him to serve them. In a couple of years, however, when Ritz was barely twenty, the Franco-Prussian war broke out. The Siege of Paris put a stop to luxury living although Bellenger did his best. He bought, for example, the two elephants that the zoo had had to slaughter and it was the *Voisin* that served up that unique Paris dish trompe d'éléphant chasseur. Finally, Ritz a neutral Swiss, left Paris and did not return until the war was over and a stream of rich Americans, such as Vanderbilt and Morgan, began to visit Europe. They were different and Ritz turned to serving them, almost by instinct. He was said to be the first European to realize that Americans had to have ice-water, and to serve it, without being asked. Quickly he became a maitre d'hotel at the *Hotel Splendide* and the management were delighted to see their sales of good vintage wines start to soar. It was some time before they could discover how Ritz achieved this. The Americans, who were the main guests, were not normally wine connoisseurs.

On the other hand, Ritz had realized that they also were dubious about the purity of the local water. He had simply indicated that the best antidote was a bottle of good wine—the better the wine, the better the antidote.

Constantly in his younger days Ritz worked himself into a good position and then to widen his experience moved away even though it meant stepping down the ladder temporarily. From real success in Paris he returned to the level of waiter in order to move to Vienna. Here he worked in a restaurant near the Imperial Pavilion. When Emperor Frans Josef entertained he borrowed extra staff from the hotel. Soon Ritz was serving regularly at these imperial functions, getting to know the tastes of the great from Bismarck to the Prince of Wales, from the Czar of Russia to the King of Italy.

After the Vienna Exhibition the waiter decided again to move on, perhaps he felt time was slipping by; he was twenty-three by then.

Ritz wanted to serve the best and he could only do this to people to whom money meant little. He decided to follow the International set, among whom he was now getting known. The established pattern was to winter in the South of France and move to Switzerland for the summer.

Ritz became restaurant manager of the *Grand Hotel* at Nice for the winter and, in the summer, maitre d'hotel at Rigi Kulm the remote Swiss village famous for its view of the Alpine sunrise, where it was normal for everybody in the hotel to get up half an hour before dawn.

The young manager did well and it was near the end of his Swiss season that Ritz showed not only his flair for organization, but an ability to cope with emergencies that was essential for any man hoping to cater for pampered and spoiled aristocrats.

Central heating had been installed in the hotel before the season started, but in September it broke down. It was an icy cold morning and thirty American tourists were on their way for lunch.

Immediately, Ritz altered the lunch menu. Every dish, to the final crepes flambées, had to be hot—no salads and no ice cream. Then he sent for forty bricks and he had these put into an oven.

No other guests were expected so Ritz shut up the vast frozen dining room and had a table to seat forty people taken in to a small drawing room decorated mainly in red (these were the days before separate tables were normal in a restaurant).

Some big copper bowls, which stood in the foyer holding

palms, were taken into the room. The palms were removed and the bowls filled with methylated spirits.

When the party arrived the spirit was set ablaze and the room looked bright and cheerful. Each guest was seated and a hot brick, wrapped in flannel, placed at his feet. The party was a huge success and probably most of the Americans never knew there had been a crisis (thinking perhaps that the hot foot brick was a quaint local custom like the Spanish brasero).

In the trade, however, word of the incident got about and young Ritz was noted as a man of resource. One who noted this, with interest, was Colonel Max Pfyffer, the architect of, among other places, the *Hotel Grand National* at Lucerne, which his father-in-law owned.

The Colonel took control of this hotel a couple of years later and immediately sent for Ritz. He offered him the post as manager of the biggest and best-known luxury hotel in Europe. Ritz was now twenty-seven.

For the next eleven years he spent each summer at Lucerne and the winter in the South of France. The Lucerne hotel required a lot of attention at first for its management had grown slack, but Ritz quickly put that right. Soon the *Hotel Grand National* was famous throughout Europe for its summer season, balls, fetes, parties and concerts. Ritz was becoming a famous international figure.

There are few well-known hotel men who have been satisfied with one hotel. Adlon was one, but he was an exception; mostly they seem to want a minimum of three or four and often many more to utilize fully their administrative ability. Ritz was quite typical. When he was thirty-seven and deciding to venture into business on his own (and get married as well), he did not think of one hotel. He scraped up all the capital that he could to get the *Hotel de Provence* in Cannes, the *Minerva Hotel* in Baden Baden and also the *Restaurant de la Conversation*. Soon the Prince of Wales stayed at Baden Baden for Easter and, thereafter, came back every year. He reached a stage where he would say to Ritz "you know better than I do what I like; arrange a dinner to my taste".

And so, before he was forty, Ritz had achieved success and international fame. His little bride of twenty herself came from a family of hoteliers and she was a great help to him in perfecting his establishment. Perhaps he could have gone on for the rest of his life quietly doing that and so, whilst missing the ultimate accolades, avoiding also the ultimate personal tragedy.

However, his fate was decided when Rupert D'Oyly Carte went to Baden for the cure. He was looking for somebody like Ritz to run the Savoy for him.

In 1246, Henry III gave a stretch of land "for services rendered" to Peter, Count of Savoy. It was not entirely free— Peter had to pay an annual rent of three arrows, in return for which he got not only the land, but "all services" whatever they may have been.

In those days the Strand was a cart track running parallel to the Thames from the City to Westminster Abbey.

The Count of Savoy built himself a magnificent palace in this wooded countryside by the river. Subsequently, this came into the possession of John of Gaunt and during his tenure received its first official overseas guest of exalted rank. The King of France was captured at Poitiers and brought to London a captive. He was treated with the utmost courtesy and soon allowed to return to France, hostages taking his place, one of whom was his son, the Duke of Anjou.

To the distress of his father the Duke broke his parole and escaped back to Paris. The King felt he had no alternative as a man of honour, but to return to London voluntarily to be a captive again.

It is hard to imagine any of the world's leaders taking quite this attitude today but perhaps there was no great hardship involved. John of Gaunt lent the King his Savoy Palace where the London citizens attended with large bands of minstrels to welcome him back to captivity "with much reverence". This, he might have thought, was the way to run an Oflag but, unfortunately, he died of a chill after a few months.

The next tenant was the poet Chaucer but in 1381 the mob,

inflamed by Wat Tyler's revolutionary zeal, attacked the palace and sacked it. Again a high-minded attitude, unfamiliar today, was evident. Leaders of the insurrection ordered that there would be no looting—all the precious stones and gold were to be thrown into the Thames.

One unfortunate who tried to secrete some gold plate was thrown on to a fire to burn to death. The wine was flowing in the cellars, not all of it into the Thames, when there was a vast explosion. Rioters had thought that some kegs contained jewels and threw them on to the fire but they were full of gunpowder. The rubble trapped the drinkers in the cellar below where they "were heard crying and calling seven days after, but none came to help them out until they were dead".

After this the old palace lay in ruins until the hospital, mentioned on page 55 was built there in 1509. After the Reformation the hospital became, for a time, a naval hospital but finally it fell into disuse. When the whole area was described two centuries later it was a squalid mess of warehouses and coal sheds backing on to the embankment wharves. With the ruins and a prison there was also the headquarters of the Worshipful Company of Upholders (now called undertakers—slipping?). Here, for instance, was agreed the scale of fees to be paid to domestic servants for information about any pending deaths in their household. It was this semi-derelict waste that Richard D'Oyly Carte inspected thoughtfully in 1884.

Nearly ten years before he had started his immensely successful association with Gilbert and Sullivan. At a time when the pound was worth over five times its present value and income tax was squeezing a whole sixpence out of the wealthy man's pound, they were making £60,000 in a good year, less tax, of course. D'Oyly Carte had already invested some of his profits in the Savoy Theatre and was now considering his next venture.

He had paid several visits to America and, like most Europeans, been very impressed by the great luxury hotels there. Although there were also some fine hotels now on the Continent at the spas no European capital had any hotel to compare with the

St. Louis, or the *Lafayette,* or the *Palace,* the hotels of quite ordinary American cities, never mind places like the *Astor* or the *St. Nicholas* in New York. (The *Tremont* was by now becoming old-fashioned and only had a few more years life before it was demolished.)

London, in those days, was without doubt the capital city of the world, and obviously it ought to have the finest hotel in the world. Ten years before D'Oyly Carte had discerned what a fusion of Sullivan's genius and Gilbert's wit could produce. Now the same gift enabled him to look at the dreary wasteland of warehouses and coal wharves and see the advantage of the site.

The Savoy Hotel Limited was formed with a share capital of £200,000. Gilbert and Sullivan both joined in the venture, Sullivan as a director.

In August 1889, sixty years after the *Tremont* had opened in Massachusetts, a building seven storeys high was opened alongside the Thames, claimed to be the best hotel in the world. There were, for example, no less than seventy bathrooms. Although the rebuilt *Shelbourne* had been opened in backward old Dublin twenty-two years earlier with fifteen bathrooms the only comparable London hotel, the *Victoria,* had four. (There was a flat tin bath holding a few inches of water under each bed. It could be pulled out and filled from a can.) Water for the *Savoy* is pumped up from their own artesian well bored 800 feet through the London chalk beds; the deepest well in London.

D'Oyly Carte was a man of great imagination and foresight. When he had opened his Savoy Theatre it was the first public building in the world to be lit by electricity. Before the first performances he used to go on to the stage and smash a light bulb to reassure the audience that they need not fear a fire or explosion.

Naturally, he used electric light again throughout the hotel. According to the prospectus: "The only artificial light used over the entire building will be Electric Light, and the supply will be continuous during all hours of the day and night not only in Sitting Rooms but in Bedrooms, the button or switch in the Bedrooms being so placed that the light can be turned on or off without getting out of bed. The electric current will be obtained from a large installation in the basement of the Hotel so that the supply will not depend on any outside source . . ."

The large installation in the basement was based on a fair-engine and was completely successful. The *Savoy* was the first hotel in the world to have its own power plant and so today it has the oldest power station in Great Britain.

Not that it is in any way out of date—the *Savoy* has always aimed to be ahead of its time. For example, the generators were changed from coal to oil firing as long ago as 1919. Today the plant produces power not only for all the needs of the hotel but also for adjoining properties belonging to the company—the output would actually suffice for a good-sized town, in addition, the steam from the generators is harnessed for cooking and to heat the hotel.

In fact, for some time after the last war the Electricity Commissioners had their offices in Savoy Court so that they organized the nation's electricity resources by the private enterprise light from the *Savoy* generators. Gilbert would have liked that.

On the other hand, Oscar Wilde did not like the new electricity —it was a "harsh and ugly light, enough to ruin your eyes and not a candle or a lamp for bedside reading". In fact, there was not much he did like. "Who wants an immovable washing basin in one's room? I do not. Hide the thing. I prefer to ring for water when I need it." Also he complained that the elevators were too fast.

Six hydraulic lifts had been installed (there are thirty-two today) and were claimed by the American Elevation Company to be Europe's best and largest. These also were ready for use "at all hours of the day and night, perfectly safe, their movement smooth rapid and pleasant".

A lift in Europe was a rarity in 1889. This normally meant that no visitor was prepared to pay much for accommodation above the first couple of floors in an hotel so the higher the room the smaller and more meanly it was furnished.

Not at the *Savoy*. For the first time the upper floors were of the same proportion as the lower for, with a lift, all the floors were virtually at street level.

The building was the first in England (it claimed in the world) to be built entirely of fireproof material. Timber was used only in doors and window frames. All the floors and walls were of reinforced concrete, the steel framing being encased in concrete. (It has been bombed in two wars and yet has escaped the conflagration which has ended so many American hotels.)

This, then, was the building D'Oyly Carte prepared for his perfect hotel and this he wanted César Ritz to direct. Ritz refused. He was enjoying life very well and saw nothing in London to attract him.

Eventually, D'Oyly Carte persuaded him, at least, to come over for the opening of the *Savoy,* and offer any suggestions he might have. D'Oyly Carte hoped to give the impression that Ritz was, in some way, associated with the *Savoy,* and he tempted the great hotelier with a fee equal to his own earnings in a year as a director.

Ritz had never been to London before and was impressed by the social life. He could see that there was room for a good hotel, but he thought that there was a lot wrong with the *Savoy.* After a few months the directors agreed with him. Again they asked him to come over, on his own terms and, this time, he agreed. Quickly he summoned the best maitre d'hotel (Echenard) that he knew and who but Escoffier for chef de cuisine?

Was ever a man so fortunate as D'Oyly Carte in his associates? In the one sphere he had Gilbert and Sullivan working together, in the other Ritz and Escoffier.

His first problem was that at that time dining out in London was simply a matter of going to somebody's home—nobody dined out at an hotel. Obviously people staying at hotels ate there and might occasionally ask guests to join them, but this was due to force of circumstances, not choice.

Today nobody would consider leaving home at bedtime to go out somewhere to sleep. At the end of the last century it would have seemed equally extraordinary to anybody "in society" to leave home at dinner-time and go to an hotel or restaurant for a meal.

Men had their clubs and chophouses, of course, but when ladies ate out it was in another private house, or most ladies that is. Andre L. Simon in his *The History of Champagne* wrote: "There had been up to that time two very different sorts of 'smart' women in London, Paris, New York and other great cities: those whose heart's desire and profession or vocation was to please men, and the others: they did not mix. It was only in the late eighties, with César Ritz at the Savoy . . . that a new and much higher standard of elegance was introduced into the catering world: for the first time grand luxe and bon gout were happily partnered, and for the first time also the wives, sisters and daughters of members of the old aristocracy and of captains of industry and of wealthy financiers dined with their male escorts in fashionable public places, where they had no objection whatever—far from it—to meeting all the more glamorous cocottes of the day."

This was a real social revolution that D'Oyly Carte and Ritz achieved. It was not easy. They planned the Savoy Restaurant to be independent of the hotel, an attraction for the non-residents. There was a separate dining room for residents if they preferred and there was a small grill-room for men only.

Escoffier's French cuisine offered food unexcelled anywhere in the world. The building and decor were sumptuous and César Ritz provided a service beyond reproach—what more could the *Savoy* do to entice the Londoner? Yet at first they were slow to come and D'Oyly Carte was baffled.

He wanted to combine his two interests and introduce theatre suppers but English licensing laws prevented this. He and Ritz tackled everybody of influence they knew starting with their own customers, such as Lord Randolph Churchill, Mrs. Langtry, and Henry Labouchere. Before long the laws were amended, as necessary, so they could offer late suppers.

At that time the *Savoy* was in the centre of London's theatre-land. There were half a dozen theatres scattered around the West End and all the rest were along or near the Strand and so very convenient to the hotel. Soon even the most conventional ladies expected that after a visit to a theatre her escort would take her on to the *Savoy* where supper was served from 11 p.m. to 12.30.

This turned the tide and soon the idea of going along to the *Savoy* for dinner became more accepted, although it was still the usual thing for dinner parties to be held in private houses right up to the First World War.

People like the Prince of Wales and the Comte de Paris knew and trusted Ritz. If the *Savoy* was good enough for him they were prepared to try it. Soon the restaurant became famous for its company as well as for its food.

Ritz was able to maintain strict standards. He insisted on evening dress and banned ladies wearing hats or unescorted; to this day ladies, no matter how famous, cannot appear in the public rooms in any form of trousers, no matter how fashionable.

One of the secrets of the *Savoy's* success was a close relationship with the stage. This followed naturally from its situation and D'Oyly Carte's own associations. The hotel attracted the great names—Henry Irving lived there, Sarah Bernhardt nearly died there (from an overdose of drugs), Pavlova danced there; Lily Langtry, Dame Melba, Tetrazzini, Caruso, Chaliapin—it was home to them all. Who could resist such food and such company?

A chance, for example, to see a scene as Mr. Michon described. Michon was head of the Savoy Reception after the famous Victor and he recalled the time when Chaliapin, Maria Caniglia, Gigli and other stars of the opera world happened to be staying at the *Savoy* together. They all met in the foyer at lunchtime and marched into the restaurant singing the Quartette from *Rigoletto*.

This was not the first time the restaurant had heard good music. In his early days Ritz decided that the English did not seem to enjoy conversation during the meal as on the Continent. He thought that this being the case they might enjoy a good orchestra. In typical Savoy fashion he engaged Johann Strauss, arguing that people would linger over dinner to hear him. The extra drinks would pay Strauss's high fee.

When Ritz had agreed to come to the *Savoy* he had stipulated that he should be free to interest himself in other hotels, outside London. Now a number of wealthy business men, such as

Calouste Gulbenkian, the oil magnate, began to press him to establish a good hotel in Paris, worthy of that city.

Ritz was not at all keen to work again in Paris; his early years there had not been happy and the atmosphere of London suited him far better. However, one feature was irresistible to somebody who had left Switzerland an unknown boy thirty years before—the hotel would bear his own name.

So in 1896 the Ritz Hotel Syndicate Limited was formed. As he got the opportunity Ritz started to seek suitable premises in Paris, although he was still working for the *Savoy*. Then the following year he left London in a surprising fashion.

When Ritz arrived at the *Savoy* he came up against a house-keeper already on the staff. She disliked Ritz and caused him a great deal of trouble, but he could not get rid of her as she was evidently under the protection of one of the directors.

Eventually, after eight years, in 1897, things came to a head. Ritz gave an ultimatum: "Either that woman goes or I do". It is hard to believe that they let Ritz go and indeed it is denied now that this incident happened at all. In his *The Savoy*, Stanley Jackson says the story is pure fiction. However, this is the account of the matter that Mme Ritz gives and it is significant that immediately Ritz's nearest colleagues, Escoffier, Echenard and Agostini all resigned (subsequently to form the nucleus of the Paris staff). Lady de Gray called on Mme Ritz especially to tell her that the Prince of Wales had cancelled a party he had arranged at the *Savoy*, saying, "Where Ritz goes, I go".

It was a blow to the *Savoy* but not a fatal one; it was now established as London's leading hotel and D'Oyly Carte found the best possible replacement for the irreplaceable Ritz.

George Reeves-Smith, not yet forty, was the managing director of the *Berkeley* and had a first-class reputation. D'Oyly Carte offered him the position but Reeves-Smith explained that whilst he would like to come he could not as he was under contract to the *Berkeley*. D'Oyly Carte had no difficulty solving that; he bought the *Berkeley*.

Ritz went to Paris and soon decided that 15 Place Vendome would house his hotel perfectly. It had been the town house, originally, of the Duc de Lauzun (who led the French Cavalry at Yorktown in 1781). Ritz was seeking an atmosphere intimate and exclusive in which he could establish, as he said, "All the refinements of living that a prince might hope to incorporate in his town house".

It is quite clear from the way he phrased this that Ritz had quite a different concept from, say, the American hotel men who set out to build palaces for the people. The people Ritz intended to cater for already had palaces, from which he would have to lure them.

His backers were very disappointed with the house he chose—he was going to operate on a scale altogether too small for their ideas. They were thinking in terms of seven-storey blocks and Ritz was not even prepared to build over the gardens around the house.

It was expensive to buy an eight-day option on the property, but Ritz borrowed the money from a wealthy vineyard owner, Mr. Lapostolle, who was indebted to him. Years before Lapostolle had approached Ritz with a new liqueur he had just concocted and asked him what he thought of it. Ritz encouraged him to market it and suggested a name for it—Le Grand Marnier.

In the breathing space the option gave him Ritz tackled his backers. They thought the property so small that Ritz would not be able to get a decent profit margin out of it. He offered to guarantee them a 6 per cent return on their money in the first year (which he did).

He got his way, as he usually did; the company bought "the little house to which I am very proud to see my name attached". Ritz did not say this lightly. He had achieved success in every sphere of his profession. He had enjoyed substantial cash rewards, his views were sought by the greatest, royalty announced that they would follow where he went. The only prize lacking was an hotel bearing his own very distinctive name as, say, Sam Shepheard had in Cairo.

When he finally achieved this nothing less than perfection, in every aspect, could satisfy him—and he was a perfectionist. At a time when skill and labour and materials were readily available to those with money he spent two years preparing an hotel that was faultless in every detail.

His widow told how for weeks she had to sit, for hours at a time, whilst Ritz and his electrician tried the effects of variously coloured lights on her complexion. Electricity was new then, but already Ritz was seeking not merely light but illumination that would flatter his customers.* He also pioneered indirect lighting with alabaster urns throwing light up on to a tinted ceiling. And this was at a time when, as Mme Ritz wrote, "the last word in artistic lighting was considered to be a bronze nymph holding up a cluster of naked light bulbs in lieu of flowers".

The cabinet maker he used was equally fastidious and the rose-brocade-covered chairs, specially made for the dining room did not arrive until the morning of the opening. Ritz tried one. It was good. Then he tried it at the table and frowned. The table was too high. Two centimetres had to be cut off every leg he ordered. Impossible—they would have to be used as they were and altered after the opening, he was told.

Ritz would not hear of it. Every table had to be put right and in the end it was done, but the waiters were only just finishing laying the cutlery as guests started to arrive.

The opening was not in the American style. There had been no publicity, no crowds were sought. Just a few of the right people: The Dukes of Marlborough, Portland, Sutherland and Norfolk, for example, over from England with their Duchesses; the Vanderbilts of America, Princes from Russia and Italy, as well as the cream of French society, including Marcel Proust looking shy and nervous.

The evening was a success, partly because, as in London, the idea of ladies dining out in a public place was still a novelty.

Princess Antoine Radziwill, for instance, had been taken aback by the suggestion, but agreed to go with her nephew, Boni de Castellane and his wife. Later de Castellane told Ritz he had received a letter from her thanking him for his hospitality and

* Shortly before this—in 1889—*Punch* was quoting a recommendation that "light Japanese sunshades will be found invaluable" to ladies who found electric light unbecoming to their complexions. Du Maurier had a cartoon showing four ladies in a drawing room all holding up sunshades.

remarking "I did think it so amusing when you took me to dine at the inn".

De Castellane himself told Ritz he was going to dismiss his chef; "it is foolish to try to compete with you and Escoffier".

As soon as the hotel was established in Paris, Ritz turned his attention to the next project and went back to London.

His immediate interest was the *Carlton* in London which he completely remodelled. It was the first hotel in London to have a bath to every room, and became an immediate success. It paid a 7 per cent dividend in the first year and it was decided to build a London Ritz. The Piccadilly/Green Park site was bought but Ritz was never to see anything more than the plans.

The *Carlton* was fully booked for the Coronation in 1902, and Ritz drove himself mercilessly. The new king had been a patron from his days as a waiter in Vienna and he was determined that the *Carlton* should surpass itself.

At the last moment Edward was taken ill and had to have an immediate operation for appendicitis. The Coronation had to be postponed and all the festivities cancelled.

Ritz started to give the necessary instructions and then he suddenly fainted. For over thirty years he had lived on his nerves under constant pressure. Now, this was too much. He collapsed —a complete nervous breakdown.

Ritz was never to work again. For sixteen years he lingered on in nursing homes, his memory failing, a prey of melancholia. His wife, aged thirty-four when he collapsed, continued the day to day running of the Paris hotel. When the war broke out in 1914 he was moved to a clinic near Lucerne in his native Switzerland —a neutral country.

It was only just before the war ended, in 1918, that he had a final collapse. Mme Ritz was sent for, but it took two days to get her papers to cross the frontier. He was dead when she arrived.

The hotel world has always had its share of characters. There was Henry Bailly, Mine Host of the *Tabard,* a bailiff and Member of Parliament. "A fairer burgess is there none in Chepe," said Chaucer. "A seemly man—bold of his speech and wise and well taught." Bold of his speech too was John Fothergill of the famous *Spread Eagle*; as Robbie Ross once said he was "the worst mannered man in London, but when you know him he's far worse." (But he still had the best inn in England.)

Simeon Boyden, perhaps the first great American hotelier, was paid a bonus when he left the *City Hotel* in Boston, Massachusetts, not to run any competing hotel (so it was his son Dwight who ran the *Tremont* while pa kept a fatherly eye on it). He was called the "Prince of Landlords".

Charles Baekler went one better. He was the "Hotel King", a Swiss errand boy who bought *Shepheards* and finished up building the *David Hotel* in Jerusalem. At the time Ritz was opening his Paris hotel Baekler controlled hotels with a total capacity of over four thousand bedrooms, an astonishing figure in those days. Perhaps twice winning the 40,000 golden franc French National Lottery helped him.

Above all there was the great Sam Shepheard himself, an astonishing character. When officers of the 10th Hussars were moved suddenly and left without paying their bills, Shepheard did not bother to make an official claim. He followed them to the Crimea and went around the trenches at Sebastopol until he "settled all within fifteen shillings". When he retired, the U.S. Consul said that he "left behind him a name that is identified with Egypt and with Cairo as closely as it would have been had its owner built a pyramid".

However, who would dispute the absolute supremacy in his own sphere, of César Ritz, the thirteenth son of a Swiss smallholder, who was told, when his Paris hotel was opened "Kings and Princes will be jealous of you Ritz, you are going to teach the world how to live".

The speaker was not thinking of the world we know and Ritz was only to have four years to make his mark. But his hotel still stands and his name is still famous whilst most of the Kings and Princes he entertained are already being forgotten.

CHAPTER 10

FULL CIRCLE

I'm not Drunk,
Starkle, Starkle little Twink,
    Who the hell you are I think
I'm not as drunk as some
    thinkle peep I am.
Besides I've only had ten martinis
And anyway I've got all day
Sober to Sunday up in.
I fool so feelish, I don't know
    Who's me yet
But the drunker I sit here,
    The longer I get.

THE beginning of this century with unlimited labour available*
and an upper class untroubled by taxation, was the high water
mark of the great luxury hotel.

This was a world far removed from the inns of New England
where guests had to attend family prayers and might be put in
the stocks. This is a world where the customers' slightest wish
is law. The Savoy boasts that any guest's whim may be gratified
at 4 a.m. as easily as 4 p.m. (This might not seem a big claim
to a New Yorker, but in Cinderella-complex London it is the
ultimate.)

When Frau Adlon went into the Reception Office of her
husband's hotel in Berlin for the first time she was surprised to
read the detail in the card index of guests.

---

* Today the Savoy still has a staff of 1,550 to look after a maximum of
500 guests. In the Ritz, Paris, guests have to rub along as well as they can
with less than three staff each.

"I had imagined, like any other layman, that the reception clerks had little to do beyond allotting rooms to the arriving guests, answering their enquiries and generally being civil to them. It was with great astonishment that I found in the reception office a huge and meticulously compiled card index of which the following are a few examples.

Count X. Two pillows. Dislikes soft towels, thinks them degenerate.

Frau Meyer. Industrialist's wife. No strong smelling flowers in the room. Berliner Lokalanzeiger every morning. Hot water bottle. Dog (dwarf dachshund) called Morchen, to be taken out by a page in the mornings. Dog has breakfast with mistress. Milk and rusks. Remember to enquire after dog's health.

Schmitz. Factory owner, Selingen. Should be given a room served by an elderly chamber maid."

In the free spending days before the last war in any of the great luxury hotels it was nothing for a guest to require her suite re-decorating, perhaps in a colour to match an evening dress for a special occasion. The temporary removal or construction of walls or doors was all part of the service.

The Maharajah of Patila took the whole of the fifth floor comprising thirty-seven suites when he stayed at the Savoy in 1925. A silver bath was installed and a special kitchen built for the chefs in his retinue of fifty to prepare curries and native delicacies. A private lift in scarlet and gold lacquer was another necessity.*

There were plenty of Europeans fond of lavish ostentation, such as the gambler J. W. (Bet you a million) Gates who paid a £20 bill at the Savoy with £200 in £5 notes and waved away the change—two hundred pre-Great War pounds! Little wonder that the first Head Porter of the Savoy, Nicholas Mockett, left £40,000 when he died. (The directors had been concerned when

---

* This service provided in a luxury Western hotel is lavish by European standards, but must often seem crude to an Eastern potentate. Certainly to the Maharajah who had on his staff twelve personal shirt makers (enough to form a football team and still leave a reserve stitching away all day at shirts). What could even a Maharajah do with so many shirts?

he retired in case he might be in want and had allowed him a generous pension.)

G. A. Kessler, in particular, set a pattern for one form of ostentation. He was a Wall Street financier and champagne millionaire of severe appearance. He wore a pointed beard, gold rimmed eye glasses and looked like a bad-tempered president of a temperance league. In fact, he was an eccentric party-giver on the grand scale.

For his Jungle Dinner in New York he had real orange trees shipped from Florida and coconut palms from Bermuda, to decorate the banqueting hall. Another time he chartered an airship to dine with his guests over the Atlantic (at the beginning of the century).

It was the Savoy that attracted him most. He had been greatly impressed by the dinner given there, in the Winter Garden of course, to Commander Peary on his return from the North Pole. There was artificial snow, a model of Peary's ship among realistic icebergs on which stood lifelike penguins and bears. The waiters were dressed as Eskimoes.

Kessler decided that the party to celebrate his birthday should have a warmer motif—Venice.

The forecourt of the Savoy was flooded and reproductions of St. Mark's, the Palazzo and other landmarks were erected. In the centre was a vast silk-lined gondola to seat twenty-four guests. Twenty-five thousand carnations and roses were used in the decoration and a hundred white doves gave movement to the scene. A score of white swans should have done the same, but the water on which they were to glide had been dyed blue and this poisoned the swans. They floated about, feet upwards, until they were fished out by the waiters.

The meal was served on the gondola and the birthday cake arrived on the back of a small elephant that had to walk up the gang plank to the table. Caruso sang at a reputed fee in excess of £300 and the host was so pleased with all the arrangements that he gave nearly as much again in tips.

The next step in this sphere would presumably have been the inclusion in some hotel brochure of "Orgies specially catered for" but this never seems to have happened. The First World War and massive taxation came too soon.

It was, as usual, in America that the next real stage in hotel development occurred. From the earliest times the merchant has been a great traveller and in the nineteenth century the old article appeared in a new guise—the commercial traveller. Originally an English phenomenon and at first known as "the drummer" (he went out to drum up business) he became the American travelling salesman and almost immediately a part of the folk mythology.

The *Hotel Gazette* estimated in 1883 that there must be more than 200,000 commercial travellers on journeys around the United States but over a quarter of a century was to pass before somebody realized all that this implied.

Ellsworth Milton Statler's was a typical American success story —at least as we like to think it now. Starting work at the age of nine for fifty cents a day, he died controlling more hotel property than any man in history—the annual receipts were over twenty-five million dollars. And all because he provided a better service than anybody else.

When Statler first made some money and could plan his own hotel, he knew just what he wanted. He was not interested in the resort hotel and he could not afford, had he been interested, a great luxury hotel. What did not exist at all, and what he now saw the need for, was the commercial hotel.

He built the first one and called it *The Statler* (later *The Buffalo*) in Buffalo, N.Y. Here the small business man and the travelling salesman could enjoy a scaled-down version of the luxury hotel at a price they could afford.

"A room and a bath for a dollar and a half" boasted *The Statler* and this was exactly what the commercial man wanted. *The Statler*, opened on 18th January, 1908, was the first commercial hotel in the world, with a bathroom for every bedroom and running ice-water in them all. Here began the tradition of the free early morning newspaper and later Statler was the first to wire every room for radio.

When he died Statler was claimed to be the Father of the Modern Hotel and he may well have been. Certainly he was the owner of a large number, which he probably preferred.

One sphere in which the Americans have never given the lead, probably never wanted to, is in camping de luxe. Probably no nation has spent more time round blazing camp fires than the Americans (not mentioning, of course, the Indians in their tepees), but there has never been the great mass of underpaid peasants that are needed for camping in the grand manner.

The levels of Tiberius or Marco Polo's Grand Khan are not likely to be reached again anywhere, but fair attempts were being made in places like India even after the First World War.

Lord Frederic Hamilton has described how he was invited to a shooting party in Bengal. He arrived to find all the Maharajah's family roller skating to a Viennese waltz played by a string orchestra of thirty-five under a Viennese conductor.

"The shooting camp was an immense affair. Each guest had an Indian double tent, bigger than most London drawing rooms. Every tent was carpeted and completely furnished with dressing tables and chests of drawers as well as writing tables, sofa and arm chairs, while there was a little covered canvas porch outside, fitted with chairs in which to take the air and an attendant satellite of a tent to serve as a bathroom, with a big tin tub and a little trench dug to carry away the water."

The establishment included an ice-making machine so that when everybody donned full evening dress to enjoy dinner to the strings of the orchestra their champagne was properly iced.

There was enough real covered-wagon camping in the recent American tradition to discourage anybody playing at the game like this. If ordinary tents were not satisfactory for a few nights out of doors, the American tradition has been to erect cabins.

When motors came to America and there was, at first, hardly enough cross-country traffic to support real hotels in some places; any demand was often met by erecting simple cabins and letting them off to transients for the odd nights.

Generally they were in isolated situations where it was not possible to find staff so service was minimal and often there was no individual plumbing.

In 1924 Mr. James Vail had accommodation for motorists on

the north side of San Luis Obispo on Route 101 at the foot of
the Questa grade. He called it Motel Inn and fixed an electric
sign . . . OTEL. The first letter flashed "H" and "M" alternately
and this was the first use of the word MOTEL.

The idea of using individual tourist cabins instead of a hotel
was really developed, after 1930, along U.S. Highway 66 in the
south-west and was as typically an American idea as the
Tremont luxury hotel or the *Statler* commercial hotel.

A motel is distinguished from a hotel, according to the American Hotel and Motel Association, by its direct appeal exclusively
to the motorist. From this it follows that it is on or near a main
highway and for every room there is adjoining space for free
parking of a car.

After the Second World War the motel as we now know it first
appeared. These were one storey continuously-linked rooms in
remote locations. They were cheap to build and cheap to run
and their first great attraction was that they were cheap to stay in.

As competition increased recreational facilities started to appear.
At first these would just be small swimming pools and play areas.

The major disadvantages of the motel was the need, in the
morning, to pack up and move out to the nearest town before
any breakfast was possible. The provision of early morning coffee
then became the next step followed by breakfast. This greatly
increased the appeal to the business traveller and he is the most
important source of business for the motel.

The ordinary tourist and holidaymaker is of less importance
because his visit is usually concentrated into June, July and
August. Anybody can fill a motel in these months, the profit
comes from patronage during the rest of the year.

As a result some motels are now setting out to attract con-
ventions. Meeting rooms and banquet facilities are being added,
where suitable, not only to counteract the off-season drop, but
also in the hope that some of the guests will return for overnight
visits when they are next in the area.

The success of these various improvements is evident from the
figures. In 1963 the U.S. national occupancy rate of motels was
over 70 per cent compared to about 64 per cent for conventional

hotels. To appreciate this fully it must be remembered that motels themselves were growing at an extraordinary rate. In 1958 there were only about 600,000 units that could be classified as motel rooms. In 1963 the figure was well over a million—practically double in five years. It is estimated that motels accommodate about 325 million guests each year.

A considerable convenience for the trans-American traveller is the development of franchise chains of motels across the country. The Holiday Inn and Howard Johnson's chains set a standard which the traveller can rely upon and so individual recommendations are of less importance. Also it is very easy to book ahead or switch bookings from one motel to the next.

The latest step is the 500 room quasi-resort motels designed to attract visitors from their homes just "to get away from it all'. These have to be complete miniature resorts with swimming pools, a golf course, first-class restaurants and all in an attractive setting, close to major highways and within a couple of hours driving from a large metropolitan area.

Establishments like the Wagon Wheel in Rockford, Illinois, or the Cherry Hill Inn near Philadelphia aim to induce people to leave their crowded cities and suburbs for a refreshing break— just as Ritz set about persuading London and Paris society to leave their homes and eat out.

The European holiday camps are not the same thing—they cater for longer holidays, at least a week and usually two—and for a generally lower income bracket.

It is interesting to speculate what the toilets of Toronto might be like today if a certain stocky little South African had had his way. After what could perhaps best be described as undistinguished service in the Canadian Army during the First World War he was out of work and tried hard to get a job with the City of Toronto Town Council as a lavatory attendant. It is delightful to recall that he was turned down because of his lack of education.

In the end Billy Butlin, now Sir William Butlin, M.B.E., worked his way back to England in a cattle boat. He landed with £5 that he used to live on and set up a hoop-la stall in a fair ground at Axminster. Here he was in his natural element and he prospered quickly. He remembered seeing, back in Toronto, the early version of dodg'em cars. There was nothing like this in Britain so he scraped up all the cash he could to get the sole concession for Great Britain.

Starting from Skegness this venture flourished too and Butlin rapidly built up an extensive amusement park. It was one place where holidaymakers always felt welcome. Skegness landladies were no different from any others—it just was the custom before the Second World War for holidaymakers to get out of their boarding houses after breakfast and only to return at mealtimes (on time!). If the weather was good this was fine, but too often the showman watched wet cold families hanging aimlessly around the streets, with nowhere to go but the amusement arcades and the cinemas.

This was no holiday for a couple and their young children. Butlin remembered the big permanent camps he had seen beside the Canadian lakes. Could he not adapt that idea to suit the less reliable Lincolnshire weather? A holiday camp with plenty of covered-in entertainment?

The first Butlin Holiday Camp was opened in Skegness in 1936 by the famous star of the flying world—Amy Johnson. The total cost was £100,000, a fraction of today's annual advertising bill.

At first the camp held 2,000, but soon had to be enlarged and by 1939 the Skegness Camp accommodated 5,000.

Butlin had another amusement park at Clacton so in 1938 he opened another camp alongside this and again this was completely successful.

This was the time when holidays with pay were becoming, for the first time, the right of the British working man. Butlin's slogan was "Holidays with pay—Holidays with play. A week's holiday for a week's wage." And he saw to it that his visitors got the best possible value for their money. One feature was the first class stage shows—his first guest artist was Gracie Fields and he has never hesitated to go for the big names, whatever the cost. As a basis there are now at least 200 permanent show people in residence in the various camps and these are helped out by the famous *red-coats*. The peculiar success and atmosphere of Butlins is largely due to these *red-coats*, friendly young people, whose sole function it is to see that everybody feels "in the swing". Many an unknown has started a stage career as a *red-coat*—Benny Hill is a fine example. Not that Butlin has not made mistakes in this sphere—he told his entertainment director he should never have signed up one young singer in 1957. At £10 a week most people would have thought the undiscovered Cliff Richard a bargain but Butlin did not like the way he sang. He did not care for the four guitarists with him in the act either. They were in the same price bracket but today, as "The Shadows" they come dearer.

Perhaps, however, this was big money to a man who had employed Frankie Howerd for £3, decided he was a flop and told him he was wasting his time trying to make a career on the stage. A couple of years later he was saying the same thing to a chubby little fellow he employed as a boxing instructor at the Filey camp. As a boxer he lasted four seasons but to find stage success Charlie Drake had to go elsewhere.

Illustrative of Butlin's anxiety to look after his campers' needs is the care he has taken to provide all his camps with churches and chaplains. His senior chaplain, Canon Tom Pugh, was made Chaplain to the Queen in 1962.

Now with seven camps in Great Britain and a million campers a year, Sir William Butlin, M.B.E., is the unchallenged giant in his particular field. All this he achieved, unschooled and from a £5 capital. Had he been better educated and had the wealth of Toronto's Council behind him what lavatories might that city have had by now!

However, holiday camps, Butlin's or anybody else's, are not to everybody's taste. The growth of the "outdoor" movement in the years after the Great War has been a remarkable feature of European life. In the twenties young people especially in Germany started tramping and cycling the countryside. Very frequently the youngsters were unemployed and, in any case, the wages were very low. Camping generally provided the cheap overnight accommodation they required, but a development from this was the Youth Hostel.

Buildings of every type, from old castles to barns, were converted—usually by the hostellers themselves—to provide simple dormitory accommodation for a few coppers a night. Blankets were provided, but visitors brought their own sheet sleeping bags. They also brought and cooked their own food. The main rules stipulated that the duration of the visit would be only a night or two and that the visitor travelled on foot or cycle. Motorists and motor cyclists were not welcome.

Substitute a horse for the cycle and essentially this was the same basic accommodation that had been provided in the middle ages.

Another turn of the circle occurred after the Second World War. Originally a few residents around the Mediterranean found that they could let their villas—anything from an apartment (usual) to a castle (unusual) tends to be called a villa in this context—to sun-starved visitors from the north during the hot summer months. (When the owners were glad to go somewhere cooler.)

Frequently the services of a lowly paid maid were included, not only to do the housework, but also for shopping to lessen any language problems.

In the early days this provided an exceptionally cheap holiday for a family. In a country like Spain, with a low cost of living, a few pounds a week was the maximum charge and split among a family, it meant accommodation for a few shillings a night each.

In many ways it is an arrangement that appeals to people visiting a foreign country. They can eat what they like when they like, follow any routine that suits them and enjoy complete privacy. Demand grew quickly and soon specialist agencies were persuading local residents to move out for the season to make way for visitors (who were generally charged twice what the residents were paid).

Here again is a return to the system that had been normal through the centuries before the resort hotel was born.

One development that is quite new is the great growth of international hotel chains. There is nothing particularly American about hotel chains as such—in 1903 the Hertfordshire Public

House Trust Company was formed to buy and improve the *Waggon and Horses*, Ridge Hill, St. Albans. This was the first "Trust House" and today Trust Houses Limited control over two hundred hotels, usually in the two or three star category, throughout Britain. In America there are estimated to be about two hundred hotel chains of all sizes, up to the hundred-and-fifty-hotel Sheraton Group, which in total own about sixty per cent of all American hotel rooms.

Conrad Hilton formed the ambition to girdle the earth with a chain of Hilton Hotels where visitors of all nations, but especially Americans, could depend on certain standards; for example, of hygiene. Inevitably this means that the world traveller tends to find one part of the world very much like another part—if they are both Hilton Hotels. As Charles Graves says in his *Fourteen Islands in the Sun*.

"Those Americans, therefore, who have not travelled a great deal, are sometimes inclined to feel that if there is any excitement in any part of the Caribbean it is liable to flare up throughout the archipelago. If, however, there is a Hilton Hotel, it means that at least the touristic flag is flying, even if it is not the Stars and Stripes. It is one of the curiosities of modern times that whereas a century ago the Americans were the great pioneers of the world, risking their lives and those of their families in the great saga of the trek to the West, despite murderous Red Indians, drought, impassable rivers, and all the terrors of the almost completely unknown, their descendants are by no means so adventurous. Many of them seem to prefer a very well-trodden path for their holidays. And a Hilton Hotel is the guarantee that they will feel comparatively at home whether or not they are used to tropical sunshine, strange dishes, unintelligible patois, outlandish drinks, peculiar rituals, and in fact a totally different way of life."

Even so an effort is made to have each Hilton reflect the life of the country it is in. Thus, the London Hilton (featured on the jacket of this book) has a typical English bar downstairs, where in an ill-lit, gloomy atmosphere the earnest traveller can drink beer as warm and flat as could be found anywhere in London. Japanese hotels traditionally have walls of oiled paper with similar sliding doors. Naturally the plate glass doors in the lobbies of the Hilton Hotels are controlled by the electric eye so that they open automatically as a guest approaches. In Japan, however, the doors do not swing open, as elsewhere. Here they slide open.

As many local staff as possible are always employed and every consideration is given to local susceptibility. When the Romans complained that the Cavalieri Hilton ruined the view of the hill on which it was erected, Hilton had a new higher hill created, to hide the first. It was tastefully done with instant maturity provided by a little copse of thirty-year-old trees costing £1,000 each.

Without doubt Conrad Hilton has opened more hotels in more foreign places than any other man in history. He enthusiastically maintains the American tradition of the big sensational opening, although even with his expert organization there is always danger of some hitch—the earthquake in 1956 when the marquee outside the new Nile Hilton was blown twenty miles into the desert— the drought in Hong Kong when the hotel could hardly function at all. Just as the Cavalieri Hilton was to be opened in Rome, Pope John died and the ceremony had to be postponed leaving the chef with 1,200 desserts on his hands; desserts of peaches stuffed with ice cream wrapped in batter and baked lightly with crushed almonds.

Perhaps the most harassing event of all, because nerves were kept on edge for so long, was the opening of the Berlin Hilton* in 1958 in the very week that Khrushchev had told the U.S. to get out of Berlin. Great difficulty had been experienced in getting a pass for a dancing bear to cross from Eastern Germany. This bear had been hired to perform in the ballroom for the opening gala. Eventually he got his visa and duly appeared but in the middle of his act the bear smelled pheasant cooking in the kitchen. He broke away from his trainer, galloped towards the pheasant and sent terrified cooks leaping for their lives.

In a control room behind the scenes an organizer fulfilling virtually the functions of a theatrical producer was wearing ear-

* This is not the Heil Hilton, that's in Munich. (It has been a pleasant game for some time to rename Hilton Hotels—the Tiltin' Hilton in Pisa, the Hilton-Hilton in Baden-Baden, the Comrade Hilton in Moscow, etc.)

phones and trying to synchronize the activities of the waiters, lighting engineers, entertainers and so on.

"There is a bear loose inside the kitchen," someone shouted to him.

"The hell with bears," he bawled, "get those salads out there on the tables."

However, nothing in the worst Hilton nightmare could compare with the opening of the *Shamrock Hotel* in Houston, Texas. J. B. Priestley gives a superb account of this in his *Journey down a Rainbow*. There had been such a publicity build-up that on the actual opening night there were literally thousands of guests, visitors and spectators in an uncontrollable mob.

"For waiters and diners it was an inferno: soup, drinks, coffee were knocked or swept off trays, to spill over the guests; at one important table, jammed with millionaires' wives, a whole tray of fruit cocktails, appropriately called pineapple surprise on the menu, was scattered over bare shoulders. One waiter, weary of being screamed at, replied to an order: 'Sorry, I don't work here. I work four blocks down the street. I just got caught in the mob.' Guests were still being served dinner after midnight. Speeches that should have been made at the beginning of the evening, by the Governor, Mr. McCarthy, the film stars, had to be kept until the end, by which time it must have looked as if a cyclone had swept through the building. (The two trees in the lobby had been stripped of all their orchids much earlier.) The Haroun Al Raschid of this Arabian Night, Mr. McCarthy, was driven to confess: 'I'm kinda peeved about a few things.' But the final word must be left to the South-western Bell Telephone Company, which, after coldly considering its statistics, announced on the following day that the opening of the *Shamrock,* regarded as an emergency operation, ranked with the Texas City disaster and the Galveston Flood."

No effort had been spared to make the event successful—each lady had even been presented with shamrock decorated panties. The total cost of the opening was said to be a hundred thousand pounds; exactly the amount that the whole of the first Astor cost (but that, of course, allowed nothing for ladies' underwear).

INDEX